Will You Be with Me?

Mother Mary's Extraordinary Invitation

www.ppp-publishing.com

Words of Love for *Will You Be With Me?*

"If ever there was a book infused with hope and love that could shift humanity's trajectory, this is it. The divine light of Mother Mary and Samarah radiate from the pages and illuminate a pathway to discover our own soul's essence. Both an intimate story of Samarah's relationship with Mary and a beacon for our own spiritual quest, she pulls back the veil to reveal our true divinity. By teaching us how to release from our own bondage, you'll be inspired to create your best life and project that light into a spiritually hungry world."

Mary Elizabeth Smith -- Founder/Host of "Heavenly Encounters" and "Health & Harmony" radio.

"An authentic Marian channel, Samarah sounds the clarion call for lightworkers to be the hands and feet of love in this world. It's GO time!"

Elaine Christine, author, *The Peace Prophecy* trilogy

"It is rare indeed to find a work that can touch the reader deeply enough to bring tears of joyous recognition and purpose on the first page. This one did."

Richard Meyers NV

ISBN: 978-1-7376603-3-0

Published by Powerful Potential & Purpose Publishing.
Book and cover design by Allison Chick.

Printed in the United States of America.

First printing edition 2021.

To the lovers and the dreamers, the singers, and the dancers. To all who share joy and lift us to the light. Thank you for inspiring us to share our gifts.

Table of Contents

Section 1:
Discovering our Light

The Light We Bring

A golden stream of light reaches for you, welcoming, incandescent, timeless. It has always been with you. It will always be with you. Shimmering, calling to you, it invites your soul to remember. It invites you to restore your lost innocence. It invites you to awaken to the power, purpose, and passion you came to earth to share. It reminds you that you are not alone, you have never been alone.

You may have simply forgotten or been misled, hurt, rejected, betrayed. The light is still here. It is still vibrant, pure, unsullied. Set aside all that has disrupted you, just for this moment, and allow the light to pour into every wound. Fill yourself with the love that has never left you. This golden stream is your connection to Source, God, Goddess, Buddha, Atman, Universe, whatever you call the force of love.

After years of longing and searching, I found my Home in the arms of the Great Mother. There I could rest. There I felt peace. There I knew the depth and breadth of divine love filling my body and illuminating my soul. I share my journey with the hope it may help you find and welcome your unique luminous light and experience the rapture such a reunion brings.

This is the story of how I found light and experienced the full range of unconditional love. For all who wander and wonder, for all who wish and dream, I offer it as my testimonial to the vast resources and miracles that abound once we connect with the kingdoms of light. If my story brings you comfort, I rejoice. If it is not for you, I also rejoice in your clarity to know what is right for you.

Called by the Light

Do we each have a destiny waiting? Are angels and guides poised to help us? Is there an invisible Path we can find? Stirred by these concerns, I closed my eyes and asked to know the answers. A scene opened up in my mind's eye and I saw the exquisite Celestial Garden where Jesus and Mary walk.

In the quiet beauty of the garden, where beloved souls come to rest between incarnations, Mother Mary walked with Jesus. Troubled by what he saw on earth, he gazed downward and wearily spoke to Mary. There is too much division, too little compassion. They blame each other for the ills surrounding them. The Emissaries who agreed to incarnate hold back, uncertain, afraid, daunted by the magnitude of the challenges they face.

We must send them an Invitation to Remember. We must remind them not only of their promises, but of the legions of light here to assist.

I told them all that I could do, they could do. They did not believe me then and they still do not believe me. The religions of the world, birthed in wonder, became steeped in limitations and misunderstandings. I taught love. I encouraged all to honor each other and bring forth the gifts they brought to share. I offered miracles achieved through the power of faith.

Dearest Mother, will you reach out to them again and visit those who are ready? There are brave souls who are not fearful, simply reluctant. Reach out to those Emissaries and invite them to step into the Path of their promise. Once they remember and can trust and find their way, their example can help others to gain the courage required to move past this ancient wound.

Mary nodded, lost in thought. I hear their prayers and am grateful for the rosaries and devotions and yet they do not choose the Path of Light. They beseech me to change their lives. Why do they blame the Creator when it is their choices creating these consequences? It is time for them to remember and have the courage to choose the light they bring to guide their way.

I see those who are ready. This time I will go not as an apparition, but as a Presence. I will walk with them. I will send out a Clarion Call to all who are searching. For those who are ready and listening, I will appear to them and ask for their willingness to help create and fulfill our dreams for humanity. They must now trust their own power.

Jesus took Mary's hand, gazing back to his time on earth and reminded Mary, What holds them back is a cellular memory. A deep wound of fear continues to thwart their desires. Their earthly bodies still hold the memory of my suffering. They fear speaking out, living a life of love, will result not only in condemnation and judgment but also in a painful death. Subdued by these fears, they wait for a savior. They wait for a hero. They do not recognize they can be the ones they are waiting for. When the human story of power as subjugation can be shifted by unconditional love, each one becomes a chalice of divinity, and the New Earth can be born. The star that guided the Magi to me is here for each of them. It is time they welcome the soul star chakra that holds their divine promise.

Mother Mary nodded. They want more proof of our love. They want proof there is a higher way. The Emissaries of Light who chose this time to return to earth must now remember and move past these ancient fears if the world is to become what we all have dreamed. I will go. I will find those ready to awaken. I will invite them to Be with Me. I will send out this proclamation for all who have ears to hear. I will offer seven gateways to free their bodies from fear and connect with the soul star that holds their divine promise. Will they open? Will they trust? Will they say yes?

Standing strong with Jesus by her side, Mother Mary raised her arms and transmitted an invitation to humanity and the Emissaries of Light. It was a call I would hear from the comfort of my living room, as I sat meditating and yearning for connection.

Mother Mary's Invitation

To all of my beloveds,
It is time for you to stop praying to me and instead join with
me to change the world that has lost its way. I ask of you to
not only love my son but embody his promise to you. He told
you all the many miracles he could do, you could do,
and more. It is true, and it is time.

All around you is the evidence of a world lost from its
Creator and from the Source of love from which you came.
Floods and fires, earthquakes and
tsunamis, devastation, and pandemics, are not the
punishment of a vengeful God. They are the signs of a world
which has lost its balance and does not live in harmony and
appreciation of all that has been gifted to you.

Brother against brother, rich against poor, one religion
against another, one tribe decimating another; all of this
turmoil stems from greed and the wrongly held belief that
it is your brother who keeps you from that which you seek.
This is a devastating misunderstanding of love and the right
use of power.

Will this be your legacy to your children and grandchildren?

Is this what you came to create?
You are the Emissaries of the Light. You are the hearts and
hands of my love. Eons ago, you made a promise to come
when there would be the most to lose and the most to gain.
Now the time has come, and I call your promise due.
No one else carries your light. It is the gift within that is yours
to summon and to share.

It is time to go forth and give what you have to offer.
Center yourself in peace.

Choose to be fully aligned with the promise you came to
fulfill.
Feel the dreams of this earth within you
ready to be born.
Allow yourself to be filled with the promise and possibilities
of your dream. Now take a breath and take the first step
toward what you know is yours to offer. Receive these Gifts
of Light and offer the gift of your light. You will not fail. It is
time and
I am with you.

Longing for the Light

There are wondrous gifts available when we listen to
that still small voice or sometimes the nudges from the other
side. Have you ever felt the tender touch of a higher source?
Are there little whispers from above that you hear when you
are quiet? Do you feel you are meant to live a different life?
I know I have felt and heard these whispers since childhood.
After years of fighting my gifts, one day it all changed. It had
to!

Angels speak to me, and guidance comes from those
who have passed over. I did not knowingly ask for this gift,
but it is something I have learned to accept. I hope by sharing
my wake-up calls, the events and people who serendipitously
and sometimes insistently arrived in my life, you may become
more aware of the inner guidance reaching out to you. You
may be an Emissary of Light ready to fulfill your divine
destiny.

Throughout my childhood, I wanted to matter. Surrounded by cheerful, confident school mates, left me feeling separate and confused. Born into a typical middle-class family, my school years were spent in Massapequa, a quiet Long Island suburb. In my family, love was not offered freely. Approval was grudgingly meted out if I completed one of my never-ending chores. The family motto was get good grades, be a good girl, do not ask too many questions and fit in.

What was challenging about this idea of fitting in was the parameters were never clear. Neither the smartest, nor the prettiest, a klutz at physical sports; what could I do to win the affection of my family or the admiration of my peers? I watched the athletes gain the admiration of the students and the teachers. My beloved art teacher, Ms. Canner, never chose my drawings for display. Invisible, unworthy, and unlovable; I wished for something, someone, to reach through the haze and see me. I longed for a light I had never known and yet believed was out there somewhere.

As a little girl, I could hear sounds and voices, like a frequency on a radio in another room. It was soft and I could not always understand what was being said. Was this simple loneliness or my grand imagination? Realizing I could turn up the sound and listen to a particular frequency of the broadcast coming through, angels and souls from the other side spoke to me.

When I was nine, we lived near a cemetery. To escape from my mother's endless demands, I would walk to the cemetery grounds with a book. There I would sit under one of the ancient trees or lean back against the headstone of a long-gone soul. Sheltered by the tree or warmed by the stone, I would gaze up at the sky, bewildered by the inconsistencies and cruelties of this life, and my "friends" would come. They spoke to me in whispered stories. They surrounded me and embraced me with their love and their laughter. I felt peace and the loneliness of my life would ease in the magic of these visitors from the other side.

From the joy of these early encounters, emerged a belief in a Presence beyond the everyday five senses. A special kingdom lay hidden just beyond my normal sight, within the ancient trees or hovering in the twinkling starlight sky. Struggling to connect with this elusive place, I dreamed it could brighten my life and expand my world. In this kingdom, I would have a place and I would belong. I kept searching for what would reveal that special kingdom. My spiritual search took diverse roads, some full of joy and learning, others disappointing and disheartening. What worked well for others was not always the Path for me.

How could I unleash my inner light and discover the luminous light called God? I studied the Course in Miracles. I went on retreats with renowned spiritual teachers like Wayne Dyer and Caroline Myss. I spent hours in nature and read hundreds of books from Alice Bailey to Tom Kenyon. Each teacher offered seeds of knowledge and comfort. I meditated, chanted, prayed, and journaled, yearning to hear what seemed just beyond my reach.

Where were the others who shared a devotion to Spirit beyond any religion? Ram Dass, the Harvard professor, now spiritual teacher, led retreats in the old-growth redwoods of Oregon at a retreat center called Breitenbush. Spiritual seekers would gather in a community setting we lovingly called "Spirit Camp." We hiked amidst the ancient trees, chanted the Hanuman Chalisa, meditated, and shared our vision of a world we could almost see in those moments of community and bliss.

During one of his talks, Ram Dass read "The Bodhisattva Vow." Tears of longing flowed as I felt the possibility of being of service in the world.

May I be a guard for those who are protector less. A guide for those who journey on the road. For those who wish to go across the water, May I be a boat, a raft, a bridge.

That day, I took this vow as my pledge and my promise. This prayer guides my choices to create a world in harmony, a world where the power of love has replaced the love of power. Yet, despite doing my best to live this sacred vow, there was still a vast chasm between the world I lived in and the world I dreamed of. What more could I do? The answer came in a radical and most unexpected way. I learned I had a destiny as part of a group of souls who had promised to incarnate as Emissaries of Light.

Visited by the Light

Mother Mary arrived in my life in an unexpected and surprising series of personal visitations. Her first appearance was in September 1997, a fall day like any other, blue sky, warm temperatures, and quiet in my newly built home in Scottsdale, Arizona. My home was serene and temple-like, with statues of Buddha and Kwan Yin. The view outside my window of the budding Palo Verde tree with its glorious yellow blossoms contributed to the beauty and calm I had worked so diligently to create. I had taken to meditating in the afternoon, after the busyness of the morning chores and activities.

I would realize I had been preparing for this moment since my childhood encounters in the cemetery. There had been early signs my life would not be "normal' and yet my day began as usual. Gratefully, I sank into my favorite chair, white leather with a hassock where I could put my feet. As I closed my eyes, the conscious feeling of peace came, and I began the comforting chakra meditation. Inwardly, I repeated the familiar words, "I now prepare to center myself. Closing my eyes for peace and calm, straightening my spine to stimulate energy flow. Opening my hands to receive, I let go and allow the light of God to fill me. The first color I visualize is red, relaxing my body from head to toe. I allow the light of God to stream through me and restore my energy and passion. I am safe." Continuing with the meditation through each of the chakras and ending with the violet at the crown chakra affirming, "I now allow the light of God to flow through me and open to experience whatever I am meant to experience."

Instead of the usual deepening peace, I felt a thickness in the room's air, as if storm clouds had arrived, charging the air with electricity and power. I sensed a huge energy presence, azure blue, feminine, perfumed, and powerful. She felt "BIG" and commanded my complete attention. Sitting up to greet this guest, I felt a lovely sweetness. Sending a telepathic greeting of respect, I asked, "Who are you?"

The presence held my heart and mind and sent back a loving message full of kindness. Many call me Mary. I knew immediately she meant Mother Mary, the Blessed Mother of Jesus. Puzzled why she would come to me; I had no previous devotion or even interest in her. Again, I sent an inner question to her, "What can I do for you?" There was a pause, and a focused centering of the energy. Her words held a tenderness I had never known as the message touched a deep place in my heart: Will you BE with .... me?

What "to be" with Mother Mary meant was puzzling.

Simply embraced by the love and sweetness of her presence, I nodded my assent. She hovered quietly in the room, and I felt a deep peace and a palpable richness, like being wrapped in a blanket of soft light. She stayed in the room for about twenty minutes. There were no more words, simply the comfort of a sweet, still silence.

Then she left as quietly and softly as she had come. I sat for a few minutes, feeling nourished by the energy she had brought. Reluctantly, I stood up in disbelief at what had just occurred and what it meant.

My mind worked to make sense of this. Why would she come to me? I had not sought her out, nor did I have a devotion to her. I had a Christian background, but no particular relationship with Mother Mary. When I asked, "What can I do for you?" she had paused, choosing the words best suited to convey her wish, Will you BE with me? She emphasized the word "Be," what could that mean?

I thought this might be the end of our encounter. I knew of the Mary apparitions and sightings; they occurred and then often-times stopped. I did not know why Mother Mary would have chosen me and stopped by for a visit. I simply felt blessed and attributed it to all the love I had lavished on this house in making it a place of love and a spiritual refuge for those who visited.

Embracing this magnificent visitation and blessing I received, I decided to keep it a secret. This world has not been kind to those who have a gift of hearing voices from the other side. I did not want to tarnish the memory of the blessing and the beauty of the visitation I had received.

The very next afternoon, relaxing in my favorite chair, with a vase of red roses on my altar in honor of Mary, I focused on my chakra clearing meditation. Suddenly, there it was again. The powerful essence of a blue cloud filled the room with the presence of Mother Mary. She seemed amused at my surprise to see her again.

Surrendering to the experience, I wondered what she might say. She simply communicated, I greet you and ask again, will you be with me? Nodding my assent; we sat together for about twenty minutes. Our exchange reminded me of the passage in "The Little Prince" explaining to develop friendship you have to come at the same time every day to allow for trust to develop.

Feeling both blessed and a little puzzled when she left, I wondered why she had said nothing after her first question. What could she want? Why would she come again to visit me? Was this encounter some kind of foreshadowing of a change in my life? I was puzzled, curious, and uncomfortable with not knowing what her continuing presence meant.

A pattern unfolded. I would sit in my special chair, light a candle, and do my meditation and centering. A few minutes later, she would arrive, and we would simply BE together for a numinous twenty or thirty minutes. Then, as if she had another appointment, she would quietly leave, and the stillness would remain. I looked forward to our time together and prepared a special altar with fresh roses in a crystal vase, surrounded by my favorite crystals, candles, and pictures.

Growing increasingly accustomed to these visits, I was now peaceful and eagerly looked forward to our reveries. What a wonderful gift to be loved in this way. Still, I wanted to know what was the reason she came to ME? It was time to clarify just what these visits were about.

I reached out to her with my mind and asked, "Why have you come to me?" I was nervous, not sure of what special reason or skill would have attracted Mary's attention.

I came to you because you were listening.

Oh, just listening. No special characteristic, just showing up and paying attention? Disappointed, I took it to mean I could have been anyone not otherwise occupied. Mother Mary studied my slumping body, my arms crossed in defeat. She knew what I was thinking and felt my disappointment. I wanted to be special, chosen for a reason.

As I struggled with my emotions, I quickly learned when you are with Mother Mary, you cannot hide your feelings or your heart. She knows everything.

Daughter, you were listening. Your heart and mind are open to helping bring the world the messages of peace and love I would offer. Your gift to hear us was bestowed on you to be a bridge between the worlds. Long have you journeyed, helping and healing as you could.

Now I would offer what comfort and knowledge I can bring. Together, we can begin to break through the barriers keeping my children from their greatness. You and I have been together countless times. You walked with me at the time of Jesus. You came at this time to bring the messages of love and blessing Jesus offered to again be expressed. You are one of the Emissaries of Light. Will you be my voice and share the messages I would offer?

After a time of silence, she touched me gently and took her leave, knowing I would need time to sit with what had just occurred. Still, I did not yet share what had occurred. I needed more time with Mary and more time to strengthen my resolve and to allow this process to become an integral part of how I would live.

I told no one. I thought Mother Mary's presence was to fill a deep space in my heart from having had a mother who, as a scientist, scoffed at my love of fairies and other realms. As a child, the few times I had tried to share my joy at hearing these messages, my mother had responded with sarcasm and scorn. I learned not to share my special world with anyone in my family. I held my counsel and simply knew these messages from the other side were profoundly real to me.

As the first month ended, just when I was comfortable with my secret encounters, Mother Mary brought in a challenging request. She entered, as usual, on her thick blue cloud of infinite light and deep presence. As we sat together in the stillness of the afternoon, Mary issued her request, Daughter, it is time for you to share with others what I would have you tell the world.

My mind flooded with doubt and fear. Images cascaded through my mind like a swarm of incessant bees. I felt Mary waiting. I felt her love. I felt my heart. I knew once spoken, there was no turning back from this agreement. A soul agreement is not a simple promise. Once I said yes, my whole life as I had known it would be reshaped. Being a Messenger of Mary would transform every molecule in my body and guide every decision I would make.

The full weight of what this might mean flooded my brain with images of crowds in lawn chairs outside my house waiting for Mother Mary's next message, rosaries in hand. My privacy would be gone. I preferred living behind the scenes. I cannot do this, I thought. Again, as always, she knew my heart and thoughts better than I did. She simply waited.

I closed my eyes, overwhelmed with emotion. Triggered by Mother Mary's invitation, the idea of being in the spotlight brought back a painful childhood memory. My older brother developed polio when I was six and he was seven.

The disease struck hard, leaving him with leg braces and impaired motor movements. He stuttered so badly my parents could not understand him. Heartbroken, I became his protector from the cruelty of the other children and his translator. I intuitively knew what he wanted, and my parents were grateful for my help.

This newfound role left little room for me to discover my own desires and talents. I loved dance class and the joy of moving my body to music and mastering the simple choreography I still found challenging. One night, eager to show my parents the routine I had finally mastered, I dressed in my favorite costume: black and orange satin with a ruffle at the top, daringly revealing one bare shoulder. Black patent tap shoes with a grosgrain ribbon bow completed the outfit.

Carefully, I made sure every detail was in place. I took a breath and shouted, "Mommy, daddy, get ready here I come!" as I started the forty-five record playing "The Good Ship Lollipop." Tapping my way into the living room, I swung my arms in time to the beat, beaming with joy and hoping they would be proud of my accomplishment.

Suddenly, my mother grabbed my arm and pulled me out of the living room. She was terribly distraught. "Don't you know how upsetting this is for your brother? He cannot walk without braces, and you waltz in, dancing away in your tap shoes. You are selfish and thoughtless. Go to your room and take off your costume now." Defeated and ashamed, I believed my shining, my being in the spotlight would hurt those I loved. This belief kept me holding back and hiding my light for years.

Opening my eyes, the memory faded, and I was back

in my living room with Mother Mary. Daughter, what is it you fear? I told her I was afraid to tell people Mother Mary had come to ME as people would be indignant, or jealous, or demanding. I would constantly be fending off attacks of anger or crowds wanting me to solve their problems and heal their wounds. I would have to give up my privacy and no longer would my life be my own. All of this I shared with her. Mary waited, taking in all my distress, until I was quiet. She left without another word.

Determined to find a way out of this assignment, I searched for an excuse to show Mother Mary I was not the right choice. I was aware Mother Mary was associated with Catholicism and held a special place in the hearts of Catholics. I thought I had found a viable reason to get out of her request. When she arrived in the afternoon, I broached the subject of why she would have chosen someone who was not Catholic and who had not shown her any previous devotion. As usual, I did it with my own preconceived prejudices showing through painfully. I gazed in her direction and offered earnestly, "Mother Mary, I think you have chosen the wrong person for this mission." She seemed to smile and asked, Why do you believe so, my daughter?

Looking down at my lap, I offered, "I was not raised Catholic."

I felt her gaze and her amusement at my backpedaling. Daughter, she said with amusement, Neither was I! I had to laugh. Of course, she would have been raised as a Jew. Still,

I searched for a way out; certain I did not deserve this honor and cautious about what might unfold from this experience. Mother Mary felt my discomfort. She reached into my heart and communicated a new way of seeing a soul agreement.

Each Emissary of Light has a divine destiny and yet your free will determines the manner in which you accomplish it. It must be a way of joy for you. Daughter, do you not yet know you choose your soul's manner of expression? If there are things you do not wish to have, then you will not choose them. When you know what you do NOT want, then it is time to create and choose and affirm what you DO want, as then you will bring it to you.

Take your time and create an agreement in alignment with the life you see for yourself.

That I could create my own soul agreement was a new revelation. The weight of knowing each word chosen would combine to form an energy signature that would draw to me the matching opportunities and experiences demanded clarity. What would be my joy? I loved being a guide and helping people find hope and meaning. Would channeling Mother Mary touch people? What kind of life could result from this remarkable and unusual gift that did not involve lawn chairs and noisy crowds?

After several restless nights, I woke up knowing the agreement I could embrace. I could not wait for Mother Mary to come, so I could tell her.

Humming my favorite song, "Mary Did You Know," I cleaned the house, banishing any dust bunnies to prepare for our meeting. With my new soul agreement, my life Path would now unfold in ways I could not predict or control.

When she came, I could feel her smiling at me. It was as if she already knew what I would tell her and was happy I had come to it myself and felt such peace. Well, daughter, she said, Have you found the agreement you would keep?

"I have," I said, "I will go where I am invited and speak to those who would listen."

The moment I said it, I felt the universal pattern of my life shift, and like a combination lock, click open to this new powerful stream of agreement. And so, we began our work together, and I learned quickly what it means to give your life in service to your most joyful soul's purpose.

Now that you have embraced the soul star that guides you, it is time to infuse each of your human chakras with divine light. This is the alchemy that will allow you to be the radiant light you came to be. Each gateway carries a gift and a sacrifice as you let go of the world's conditioning and demands and choose your soul light.

Section 2

The Gateways
THE FIRST GATEWAY:
Awakening Your Light
Root Chakra
The Sacrifice: Safety
The Gift: Courage

I Am Precious

It is not my light you seek. It is yours. No one has your precious light. It is the gift within you that is yours alone to discover, summon, and share. Let us begin.

To strengthen this new partnership, Mother Mary suggested I invite four or five close friends to a weekly evening where they could ask questions and I would do my best to channel Mother Mary's answers. Taking a deep breath, I called five trusted friends and suggested they each come with questions. Letting them know this was an unfamiliar experience for me, I asked for their support and patience, as this was out of my comfort zone.

The first night came, and I cleansed the house with sage and selected three beautiful vases of red and pink roses. The sweet fragrance filled the air as we stood together in a circle and asked for the highest good. We invited the angels of heaven to be with us and bless all we would create. I readied myself, not sure if I could bring Mother Mary's wisdom through my voice as all the previous conversations had been in a private telepathy between us. Would I be able to speak as her channel? I was not sure, but I took a breath and offered my prayer to be a clear channel for the highest good and for Mother Mary. We had a cassette tape recorder to capture every word. I nodded to invite the first question.

"Why have you come now and in this way?" I could feel the pause in the room. I could feel my heart beating, wondering what would come. Channeling requires surrendering and being patient to allow for the process to take place in its own way and in its own time. With my eyes closed, Mary's presence first surrounds and then infuses me. Slowly, she moves through my body, pushing me aside, displacing my energy with hers. I become a witness, hovering just outside my body, aware of all that is occurring, and yet not knowing what Mother Mary will say. Her voice, word choice, and cadence are unique, clearly not mine.

Remedies are why I have come. You call them "miracles" and yet they are simply the frequency required to restore wholeness. When there is a dilemma, a problem, an area in the world that seems lost in shadow, sending a concentration of light can illuminate and dissolve the shadow, creating the shift in light that you call a miracle. In every situation of disharmony or shadow, there is a remedy of love that does not require warring one aspect against the other. Remedies embrace all energies, allowing what has been in shadow to be illuminated and therefore transformed.

When you know how to navigate the realms of earth and light, you can call to you all you require. What has been forgotten for too long is who you really are. You rely on "proof" and "rational" cause and effect. Are you not also made of light? Do you not also have energy coursing through you to transmit and receive?

I have come to remind you of what you have lost and forgotten. I have come to teach and to share and to assist you in growing in grace. I have come that you might be the divinity which is yours to be. The healing balm of your light penetrates the clouds of doubt and despair that much of the world lives in. This light is the essence of God that reminds all that they are worthy of love.

This is what I call "remedies." It is your legacy and your inheritance and indeed the promise you made as you chose to incarnate. You said, "I will go, I will remember, and I will bring light to the darkness I find and healing to the pain the world still knows. I will go and bring heaven to the earthly realm."

You left the unity of light, the oneness of all, and plunged into the earthly incarnation you had chosen. Somewhere in your innocence, sometime in your childhood, the pain and limitation of earthly living fractured your knowing. You endured experiences that left you fragmented and doubting your wholeness. You suffered what would be your earthly wounds.

From this, you then created a series of beliefs and behaviors chosen to keep you safe. You denied part of you because it was too dangerous and too difficult. You feared ridicule and censure and punishment of all kinds. You learned to go along to get along. And yet, there was always a part of you that knew the truth. You might have hidden it or denied it or excluded this glorious part of you from everyday life, but it would not stay hidden.

I come now to encourage you to set this part of you free. Remove the bars from the prison you chose. Open your eyes and your heart to all I would tell you, my precious ones. There are many who cannot feel, who cannot see, who cannot hear, through the veils of their despair. When you have reclaimed your light and send it as your prayer for all, these drops of golden light touch their deepest longing and invite them to know they do not walk alone.

Slowly, as Mary's presence departed, I came back into my awareness, trembling and shaken from the power of channeling. There was stillness in the room. Everyone seemed lost in thought, revisiting their early years, looking into the shadows to see when and where their wounding had occurred. We all felt the truth Mother Mary had shared. The aching desire to find our way back and the commitment to heal all we would need to heal was palpable in the room.

We shared hugs and some tears as my friends left, each of us touched and bewildered by what we had shared. We agreed to continue weekly, and everyone would prepare questions for Mother Mary. We would continue to tape the sessions and keep notes to put together a comprehensive guide for this information.

No matter what we asked of Mother Mary, she could

regale us with wisdom about everything from computers to crystals and spaceships. As the meetings progressed, we grew increasingly excited. We were happy to gather and share a potluck dinner and then move into my living room to sit and listen and be. I grew more comfortable with the process and my ability to bring Mother Mary through with clarity, without editing or interfering.

Channeling is allowing the specific frequency from another being to be tuned into like a radio dial, and broadcast through you. I chose to be a conscious channel, staying present for the process and eager to learn from what Mother Mary shared.

When asked what it felt like to be Mother Mary's channel, the closest analogy I could offer was being in a car where I had been driving and when she came, I would move over into the passenger seat and let her drive. I was still there. I could hear everything she said. I moved over and allowed her to use my memory and my body. The voice itself differed from mine, and the sentence structure and way of speaking were also not how I would normally phrase things. Her wisdom and joy created a field of light palpable to all of us.

Eager to be sure we were on track with the special blessings of our meetings, we asked Mother Mary to define our mission for this group and for me as her channel.

Dear one, it has been written for some time a return to holiness is paramount in order for life as you know it to continue to grow in grace and in love and indeed at all. The weapons of destruction: fear, greed, and insurmountable indifference are currently wielded far too often. What is needed is a whole scale return to love and to the sanity of right action taken for its integrity and understanding of the laws of cause and effect. It is not about punishment decreed from on high. It is about reaping the seeds you have sown.

What you will do is offer relief from the burden of certainty. For too long, man has functioned certain of his steps and the outcome he would have. For too long, the passions of war and domination have been the credo by which the strong survive and the weak are put into bondage. Even those who are well intentioned offer the caveats of rules and laws that are not nature, simply custom.

What this means is there is a space in the minds of men too seldom touched. It is the space, the luminous holy space, between thought and deed. When one has the opportunity to see how thought penetrates the very ethers and causes what has been conceived to begin to form, there is an opportunity to change the thought and therefore the pattern and therefore the outcome.

If man can learn to pause and take a breath in the space of creating, his heart can begin to alter the destructive and outmoded habits which would otherwise take hold. In the pause is the divine breath of God. In each pause is the holy nature of love. In the pause is the chalice grail revered for thousands of years. It is the cup of Christ's consciousness, which is the divine manner and the divine matter underlying the human construct.

What you bring, dear daughter, is this divine pause. Your presence and your light joined with mine carry the chalice vibration and the healing waters of Babylon. You stand in the clarity of your love and the certainty of divine love courses through you. Then, the power of Spirit issues an invitation to homecoming for all.

Humbled and a bit overwhelmed with this explanation of my mission, I had hoped for something more concrete, like building a school or creating a community. Yet, the feeling of those words touched a deep place in me; the "pause." I needed to learn again the difference between being and doing. When Mother Mary had first come to me, I had asked what can I do for you? Her response had been, Will you BE with … me?

I meditated on this and asked for a vision; a way to explain this process and be a template for learning how to "pause" and see things differently. I centered myself and said my prayer and was shown how we are born full of light, clarity, and goodness. As we grow up and are encouraged in certain directions and discouraged from others, we lose our wholeness and doubt our inner authority, deferring to those around us who know the ways of the world. In my vision, I was shown we close the doors to our inner vision in order to see only as we are told to see. In the children's' story of *The Emperor Has No Clothes*, everyone pretends to admire the Emperor's new suit as he parades naked through the village until a small boy shouts out, "He is naked!"

How do we regain innocence and build confidence? We are spiritual beings having a human experience, but how do we learn to navigate between those two vastly diverse ways of being? How can we open the gateways and allow the song of our soul to become the grounding and rhythm of our life, in touch with our divinity and all the passion, promise and possibilities we came to share? We take the first step. Instead of being ruled by survival fears, the first chakra can radiate a new understanding, "I Am Precious."

Keeping that affirmation in mind, our meetings continued, I grew quite comfortable with our small group. I looked forward to these special evenings and felt we were doing excellent work putting so much of Mother Mary's messages on tape. I soon learned being comfortable often leads to the next leap! One night after Mother Mary had answered our questions, she simply said, Daughter, it is time to expand our work. I would like you to invite the public to hear my message.

Oh no, I thought, here we go again. The public! Again, my fear of ridicule and censure rose and blocked my throat. Again, Mother Mary waited for me to have my reaction and then she said. It is time. Your world needs to know of miracles and remedies and awaits your willingness to share what you have come to know.

As usual, when the next step was offered, I was reluctant, thinking of all the reasons this was not a promising idea. Who would come? What would they think of me? What if I showed up and Mother Mary did not? On and on it went, until finally I could see how fearful thoughts kept creating obstacles. To shift back into love, I meditated and breathed in the peace of Mary's love and stayed in the sacred pause long enough to feel safe. I surrendered to the next part of stepping out and agreed. When I asked Mother Mary where she would like me to do this; I had to smile at her answer. The library, she answered, It is where people go to learn.

Looking back over the last twenty years, each time I trusted and took the next step, more was revealed. Seven gifts of light would be offered, one for each gateway I crossed. The first gateway is Awareness. Here we remember we are a unique soul with gifts and graces to discover and share. The world has often trained us to follow the Path of our tribe, to fit in, to be compliant and consider others, not ourselves. We become pleasers ruled by the rewards and punishments meted out by those in charge of our livelihood.

What is our potential? What are the opportunities we could open to if we could set aside our fears and doubts? Separated from the oneness of the Creator's embrace, we awaken, puzzled and at a loss to know what has happened and why love and meaning are so elusive. Seldom are we encouraged to find our unique soul imprint or follow the celestial GPS available to guide us on our soul's journey. How can we learn to recognize the coordinates and distinguish the markers for our soul's trail? How can we unite the disparate and contradictory experiences of our life, and live the divine soul destiny we were meant to create and share?

I believe we each hold within us our soul's song, the special melody of who we are and why we have come. Remembering this song and attuning our life to the sweet notes we find is the journey from the bondage of humanity to the creative power of our divine nature. This is at the heart of feeling and knowing "I AM Precious." The Course in Miracles refers to "The Forgotten Song," saying "The notes are nothing, yet you have kept them with you, not for themselves, but as a soft reminder of what would make you weep if you remembered how dear it was to you. You could remember, yet you are afraid, believing you would lose the world you learned since then." (p.447)

That song lies within us, calling to our soul to remember. In even the most mundane lives, there are signals and signs of a higher intelligence, a loving spirit trying to reach us. We might feel urged to take a course or go to a party where we meet someone significant who changes the course of our lives. Our everyday mind wants to dismiss these moments as coincidence, mere chance, nothing special. Yet, what if there is an entire kingdom of light we could access if we would just open to an illogical and yet deeply mystical intelligence?

Religions offer a Pathway and a perspective on these realms. Yet each of the major religions suggests there is a protocol to be followed, and even an intermediary in the person of the priest, rabbi, or minister who holds the keys to the gateway. These religions often warn not to enter alone, unaccompanied, undeserving, unprepared, unworthy. You must somehow pay for your sins, do penance, or acts of contrition. Religions often teach that theirs is the superior Path to God, and anyone who does not belong to their denomination is doomed to hell. None of this dogma ever felt right to me.

Our entry through the Awakening Gateway begins when we realize we are more than our human body, more than our personality, job, or status. It may be brought on by a spiritual experience or a life crisis of some kind. Often it is fueled by a deep longing even if we have a full life in other ways.

Curious to know if Mary had felt her awakening when Gabriel first came, I asked her what she felt with that life changing message.

In truth I was not afraid. Gabriel's message matched the knowing that had been with me for as long as I could remember that my life would be shaped by the God whose presence was part of my daily breath. When Gabriel came, what I felt was, ah, so now it begins. This understanding spread though my body with a warmth of many suns. I felt a coherence that strengthened and served me through all the joys and all of the pain that was yet to come.

My special times with Mary and the wisdom and love we shared made me eager for the next gateway, where I discovered more of the destiny that waited.

THE SECOND GATEWAY:
Exploring your Light
Sacral Chakra
Sacrifice: Security
Gift: Trust

I Am Gifted

There is a special joy you will discover that marries your gifts with what the world hungers to find. What you loved as a child often becomes a way to share your light. Joy brings light to the body and awakens what has been dormant and unspoken.

We seldom burst through each gateway, eager for change. Our conditioning has led to erring on the side of safety. Worried about judgment and scorn if we try and fail, we hunker down, waiting for assurances that may never come. I was daunted and uncomfortable about Mary's request to invite the public. Yet there was something inside me, a yearning not to dishonor the gift of Mary's presence, and I wanted to follow this new Path of love.

After my initial period of resistance, I reluctantly created a flyer and booked a room at the Civic Center Library in Scottsdale, a space large enough to hold a decent size crowd. Then, still reluctant to come out in public, I did nothing to publicize it. The one lone flyer I brought to a local bookstore was put up in a back, dusty corner. With no email list and reluctant promotion, I felt certain the gathering would be small, and that was all I felt ready to manage.

Still, when the day arrived, about twenty people found their way there. Many were friends who came to support me along with a dozen people I had never seen. We began with a prayer. As I settled into the energy, Mother Mary encircled my body and filled me with light. Taking command, she gazed out at the audience and asked them to listen from their hearts. Then, as if her first sentence could be their Awakening, she spoke with a surge of power and directness:

The words of truth are seldom heard.

Mary continued by explaining we had all come as part of our soul agreement and she was here to remind us of that solemn vow.

The agreements that you made were the covenants that you swore to before you came. They were the promises held deeply in your heart and being. Some of you have already remembered and been reminded of this. Some of you are still wondering what possibility there is for you on earth. I am here to tell you that your presence is requested, your participation is needed, and your lives are required for the earth to take its next step.

Silence fell on the group as the message touched each heart. Mary then asked if there were questions.

The first woman asked about her son, who was quite

ill. Mother Mary spoke with great compassion. Death is not a punishment. It is a promise. Each of you will come home again to our love. If your son is ready for Home, we welcome him. The woman started to cry and the woman next to her reached over to comfort her.

From my personal point of view as Samarah, sitting behind the energy of Mary, I felt the poignancy of this moment and the sadness of a mother's loss. I took a breath and let it go so I could continue. An important lesson in being a clear channel is to fully surrender and allow the messages to come through without editing or interference. I did not want to be the bearer of difficult or negative news. I had to get out of the way.

The next few questions were about walking the Path and being open to disappointment and change. Then, another woman asked about her adult son, who was experiencing an autistic breakdown. He would no longer let anyone get close to him. He had lost his job and his friends. He stayed in his room all day, not allowing anyone to touch him. His mother was frantic to get to the root of it and help him if she could.

As Samarah, I held my breath waiting to see what Mother Mary would say to this woman and uneasy this mother might also receive devastating news. Mother Mary spoke quietly and directly. Your son is facing an issue arising from a past life when he did something for which he could not forgive himself. He has now created an energetic distortion within himself, so each and every loving act or word directed toward him is reversed and feels to him like a poisonous reminder of his unworthiness.

I could see the mother's eyes feeling the truth of this and yet still frightened and uncertain how she could help him. Mother Mary continued. There is a place he can go in the East where a man called Bear works with those who have similar distortions. He must go in the fall as the leaves are changing and stay for the three weeks of the program. You cannot go with him. He must go alone and work with Bear, and if your son is ready to heal, it shall be done.

Speak to Samarah after the program and she will tell you the details.

After we had finished the public questions and offered a closing prayer, the mother came to me to find out what Mother Mary meant. I took her hands in mine and said, "With all my heart, I want this to be true and I know as a mother I would do anything for my son. And yet I have to say as a woman and a new channel, I ask you to put this through your own heart and guidance and be sure it feels right to you."

The place Mother Mary suggested, the Option Institute had been founded by a couple with an autistic son. They had been told their son was beyond help and he should be sent away. Refusing the cruelty of that idea, they began the journey of finding ways to reach him. Their success and the publication of the book *Son Rise* led to the creation of the Option Institute. Just as Mother Mary suggested, there was a program in September and the mother maxed out her credit cards to send her son. I asked her to let me know how things went.

Amazing news arrived a few months later. Her son had attended the Institute and was completely healed. The work with Bear had unlocked and shifted the energy which had created the distortion. He was back to his vibrant self, working again and engaged to be married. Harriet was working hard, too. She needed to pay off the money she had spent on the program. Months later, I heard from her again. A relative she did not even remember had passed away and left her the exact amount she had spent on the program for her son.

Hearing from this mother and knowing the suggestion Mother Mary had offered through me, had truly created a miracle for this family, allowed my faith and confidence to grow. Somehow, I had been part of a miracle of healing. Reflecting on the myriad individual choices, I saw how miracles require faith and willingness by everyone involved. This mother lived in Canada and had been guided to come to Arizona. She thought she was looking for a program or healer for her son. During her time in Arizona, she had visited dozens of places, including the Edgar Cayce Clinic. Each time she left feeling disappointed and doubting how any of the healers she had interviewed could help her son. She wandered into the one bookstore where I had put the flyer. She saw it and felt something, even though she did not believe in channeling and had no particular devotion to Mother Mary.

She told me later she was at the end of her rope and had laughingly told herself, "Well, maybe this is it. When all else fails, call on the Mother of Jesus."

As my work with Mother Mary continued, I saw how important it was for me to trust and step out as I was guided in order for the miracles/remedies to occur. I reviewed the series of events which had led to this healing for the mother and her son. First, I had to agree to do a public channeling. Second, I had to show up and trust what was to be spoken would be, and whoever was to be there would be there. Third, I had to let go of any personal agenda or expectations. Harriet had to travel to Arizona and walk into the one bookstore where I had put a flyer. Then she needed to trust her feeling or impulse enough to come to the Scottsdale Library and be open to what would occur. From there, she also had to arrange the Option Institute program, pay for it, and allow her son to go without her. He had to believe in the possibility of healing.

These choices and the courage and trust of all involved led to the creation of a miracle in the life of this young man.

Mother Mary is there for anyone in the world to see if they choose to allow it. Apparitions of Mother Mary have appeared around the world and continue to inspire and mystify believers and non-believers alike. What I can tell you is seeing Mother Mary appear and having friends there with me to witness the miracle has created for me an unshakeable faith we are not alone. The unseen realms can offer us help and inspiration if we allow them to "be" with us.

The invitation Mother Mary issued to "be" with her has changed my life. I have also learned so much about the depth of love that happens when we can be with each other, without fear of judgment or reprisal. It is the gift I continue to choose and, to the best of my ability, to offer to those I meet on the Path.

In the beginning of our time together, I would often feel my own opinions and answers arise as I channeled Mary's wisdom. I saw where my beliefs would often lead me to judge someone's experience or feel that my understanding was superior to their way of seeing. Repeatedly, I would feel my own limitations and be gently shown the deeper way to offer love.

I came to feel how each person ached to "get it right" and live their true purpose. I could feel how we all wanted a magical Santa Claus approach to our wishes and how seldom we wanted to do the work that would establish that possibility. Yet each of us is made of God and our work is to remove what keeps us from that: separation, greed, jealousy, and self-doubt.
Mother Mary had a lesson she has continued to share over the years:

Your Presence is your present.

With these words, Mother Mary asks each of us to consider how our "presence" feels. Are we a positive, radiant, healthy, creative presence? Are there days and times when all we feel is anger, hopelessness, or loss? If we are to be a force for positive change and creation, then we must do the work to shift our darkness into light. Our outer experience is created from our inner state, whether that is loving and grace-filled or angry and self-destructive.

Calling upon the loving wisdom of Mother Mary, she clarified how we can create a more loving presence.

Beloved souls,

Thank you so much for your courage in addressing this issue. We see your spirit and therefore we see the light that you are. You do not always see or feel the truth of this and so we come to you this day with suggestions and ideas of how to take off the manacles and the blinders and come to soar again as the makers and the lovers and the artists of your lives.

First, what you tell yourself becomes what is true. Examine what you say to yourself about your beauty, strength, talents, health, and all aspects of your life. Notice when judgment and disdain enter your thoughts. There is where transformation and transmutation are required.

Second, build a new language for yourself in these areas. In this process, it is important to be truthful and KIND! For instance, if you have been fired from your job, rather than being angry and blaming yourself or others for this loss, a possible new way to look at this would be, "I have created a new opportunity for a more loving job. I now work in an environment that is respectful, exciting, and contributes to the greater good of all."

Third, see yourself as you wish to be seen. Know the presence that you would have, and it will be so. Allow the shifts in behavior, relationships, locale, and choices to come from the inner knowing that you will have as you align with the higher truths of the beloved soul that you are.

Last, as self-doubt and old fears come up, surround them with your love and your light. If the voice of your doubt says, "No one hires someone who...." Smile, and say, "Up until now I have not found the situation that is my match, and I now claim it as mine and allow the good of all to be my good as well."

Your presence is your present, dear ones. Let it be what you have longed for and denied. Let it be the full laughter and love and grace that you are. You might begin and end each day with the affirmation and the creative energy of "My Presence is MY Present." Let it be glorious!

As I reflected on my "Presence," I realized how much of the real me I still guarded. I worried if I said too much or shared my inner world, I might be misunderstood, criticized, or rejected. I considered what steps I could take to be more authentic and set aside my fears of being judged. I went back to Mother Mary's five steps, with the first one being what you tell yourself becomes what is true. I decided I would tell myself only affirming and loving things. My soul mantra is, "I AM a precious woman, mystical and inspiring, celebrating the joy and sacredness of all life."

It took me a week to choose the words and feel like I could say this without explanation or apology. I stood in front of a roomful of people, gathered at a weekend workshop, and proudly and loudly affirmed my new way of being. Something began to heal and shift then as I saw and felt how empowering it was to not hide anymore, to not tone down my presence to make others feel more comfortable. The entire process reminded me of Marianne Williamson's famous explanation of why we hold back.

"Our deepest fear is not that we are inadequate. Our deepest fear is that we are powerful beyond measure. It is our light, not our darkness, that most frightens us. We ask ourselves, 'Who am I to be brilliant, gorgeous, talented, fabulous?' Actually, who are you not to be? You are a child of God. Your playing small does not serve the world. There is nothing enlightened about shrinking so that other people will not feel insecure around you. We are all meant to shine, as children do. We were born to make manifest the glory of God that is within us. It is not just in some of us; it is in everyone. And as we let our own light shine, we unconsciously give other people permission to do the same. As we are liberated from our own fear, our presence automatically liberates others."

-Marianne Williamson, <u>A Return to Love: Reflections on the Principles of "A Course in Miracles"</u>

Now I had my statement, and it was time to embody it. As I meditated each morning, I would end with that statement and imagine myself as a precious light in the world. I would ask to be a healing presence and to bring me the people or situations each day where I could be a blessing. I added the personal motto I had learned in my time with Ram Dass: "May I be a guard for those who are protector less, a guide for those who journey on the road, for those who wish to go across the water, may I be a boat, a raft, a bridge."

Besides private sessions and evenings with Mother Mary, I felt guided to create group retreats and experiences. In my psychodrama training, I had learned each of us lives a very separate story. Two siblings who had the same family experiences will have vastly different interpretations and ways of looking at themselves. In order to change and heal and connect in new ways, we need to have others with whom to share and exchange our pain and our perspectives.

One of the incredibly beautiful gathering places was at a friend's home in Paradise Valley, Arizona. Spectacular views of the valley and the setting sun brought friends and spiritual seekers from all over the valley to our monthly gathering beginning with a New Year's Eve message on 12/29/99. We shared community and prayers and heard practical lessons and wisdom from Mother Mary. One of the early messages became a kind of mantra for us. In response to one person's question about what we could do to create a better world; Mother Mary urged us to "Get on the Bus."

Another monthly gathering at *A Peace of the Universe* bookstore in Scottsdale, Arizona, became a guidepost for those seeking answers on their spiritual journey. This small out of the way bookstore held such a loving energy that people would find their way there, not sure of what brought them until they walked in and felt the love and got an enormous hug from Judith, the owner and earth angel in charge.

I would show up for my scheduled night, never knowing whether there would be one person or twenty. This, too, was part of my training in trust. It took me a while to realize I was not in charge of who came. I was simply to arrive, offer my best and those who were there and who had shown the willingness to come would be the "right" ones for that night. It is so contrary to the usual success model that if I were doing this right, there would be more people arriving. Soon, I would learn about the law of attraction and see my vibratory field was being met by the frequencies that were a match for me.

The other irony was I was still doing real estate. As much as I felt I should leave it behind and follow only the spiritual Path, people I met while channeling Mother Mary, who knew I was a licensed Realtor, would ask me to help them with buying or selling a home. I would call in their guides and ask for the highest good and many times this would create their selling homes for more than the current value or finding that perfect home at a price which could not be beat.

I learned all life is spiritual when love and intention to serve are there.

So, I would channel one night and then, as I would often joke, "Slip into a nearby phone booth" and emerge the next day as the Spiritual and Professional Realtor someone needed. The joy in all of this was to see I no longer had to separate my life into professional and spiritual. I was integrating all into the life of Samarah.

Still, I kept wondering if I could improve on being a channel.

Were there other channels receiving messages similar to mine? An announcement about a channel in Reno, Nevada, caught my interest, and I signed up and booked my flight. Discovery takes us out of our comfort zones and certainly heading into a room with about eighty people from all over the world curious to hear what Archangel Michael would say thru this channel was well beyond mine!

The "I Am Mastery" workshop would allow us to become licensed teachers for this information. I was excited to learn and receive what Archangel Michael would share. As with so much of my new life, I would receive far more than what I initially imagined.

The group of eighty was a diverse and global gathering from multiple US states and several countries. The youngest were in their twenties and the oldest were in their seventies. There were more women than men, as is common for these kinds of classes, and yet because the energy of Michael was the attractor, there were about twenty men present.

Unfamiliar with the "I AM" Teachings, I had my blank notebook at the ready and chose a seat in the back of the room. Thick manuals were distributed to each of us, color coded with the seven chakras. Our teacher had been channeling for decades. Tall, stately, powerful, she held the room with her piercing eyes and invited us to stand for the opening prayer.

The room filled with a powerful energy, different from Mother Mary, and yet also full of love.

The teacher motioned for us to be seated and in a booming voice proclaimed, "I Am … Michael." At no time during the history of life on planet earth has it been more important to seek clarity and harmony in each and every moment. Every thought, emotion, verbalization, and act is being magnified and cast out into the ethers.

The information was startling and new to me. Archangel Michael talked about the golden ray and how the chakra system was being infused with a new alchemy of light. The traditional colors associated with the chakras would shift as the golden ray interacted and transformed the physical body into the light body.

I watched as Ronna easily navigated her role from leader to channel. She has a strong and vibrant presence, despite being in her seventies. She has a piercing gaze that sees into each participant's soul. Everyone was uplifted by her powerful energy and genuine nature.

Mesmerized and held by the transmission, we took notes, reflecting on just how our fears and our reluctance held back the Earth's evolutionary possibilities. At lunchtime, several participants sat together and chatted about where we lived and why we had come.

Still shy about my channeling, and determined not to hide any longer, I whispered how I had recently channeled Mother Mary. "Oh, can you give me a message, please, please, please?" one asked. I invited her back to my hotel room for privacy and she grabbed another friend and off we went. Yikes! I thought, what have I done? Here we are at the workshop of an internationally known leader, and I am going to compete? Stupid, foolish girl, I thought. Still, off we went.

As we sat in my hotel room, I closed my eyes and

said a prayer that Mary would come through, despite my discomfort. Never one to disappoint, Mary arrived and offered specific guidance to each of the women. When I opened my eyes, back in my body again, I looked at them and both women had tears of tender recognition at the love they received. My confidence was restored. Then they excitedly said, "There is no program tonight, would you offer a channeling?"

Would I do a channeling at the workshop of another channel I had just met? I knew I would need to ask her permission. Haunted by the past, I could feel the ghost of my mother and her strident voice, "Who do you think you are? What kind of audacity led you to that idea?"

Still, I was committed to stepping past the old ways of being. I saw our channel as we were gathering again after lunch. Summoning my courage, I inquired, "Some women were wondering if we could use the conference room tonight since there is nothing scheduled, and we are all staying here at the hotel?" I did not mention my channeling. That was too much of a stretch. "Certainly," she said, "just be sure to lock up afterwards."

The two women who had come to my room were beyond excited and we planned to start right after dinner. I thought a dozen might come, as there had been no announcement, just excited whispers. I had no appetite at dinner, my inner demons kept saying, "What have you done??"

After dinner, I steadied my breath, got the key, and unlocked the room, arranging the tables in a horseshoe shape. When the doors opened, about fifty people streamed in. Now what? How could I present myself to them after they had spent the day with someone so gifted? Taking some more deep breaths, I invited them to stand and say a prayer with me. As I raised my arms and asked for the highest good and all the angels of light to be with us, I grew calm. Once I let go of the frightened, uncertain part of me, a greater self took over.

Taking some deep breaths, I asked to be a clear channel for the highest good of all. Mother Mary then delivered a brief message about purpose and how to recognize when we are on track and when we are not.

One thing I noticed right away was the energy of the room was already clear and devotional. Often when I led groups, people were cautious and guarded, creating a kind of energy barricade Mary and I would have to penetrate. This time, here in this room, our host channel, Ronna and Archangel Michael, had already allayed the usual fears and doubts. Also, those who had come were already open to channeling.

They would not have traveled to be here unless they really did feel aligned with this way of learning and the channeling process.

After Mother Mary had delivered her message, she asked if anyone had a question. A man at the end of the horseshoe raised his hand and shared he had always thought he had the ability to channel, but had never been able to do it. Mother Mary asked him if he was ready to accept his gift. He nodded his assent. **Stand Up,** Mother Mary said in an extraordinarily strong and authoritative way. Reluctantly, he stood. Then Mother Mary asked everyone in the group to send him the energy and power of love. Many put their hands up to send Reiki; others closed their eyes in prayer. All the group joined with him in that moment as one heart and mind in the unified field of love.

He put his hand on his throat and Mother Mary said, "Now, Speak!" His eyes filled with tears and his body wavered as he struggled to allow both the energy being sent to him by the group, and the energy that was filling him from his guides and from Mary.

His voice built in strength, and he offered a message from Joseph of Arimathea about living as a legacy to the teachings of Jesus. Everyone in the room felt the Spirit of Joseph and continued to send light until the communication was complete. Dazed with the effort and with what had just occurred, Jim opened his eyes and looked around the room in amazement and gratitude.

Mother Mary just smiled and said, There, now you are free to channel and speak as love guides you. The rest of the group was quiet, visibly moved by the power of what had just occurred. I was reminded of Mary's first message about how we could be the remedy or miracle for others if we would allow the concentration of our light to be focused on the challenge or difficulty being presented. It was clear to me what had occurred for Jim was a remedy offered in love by the group, and I wondered what other miracles we might yet co-create.

With Jim's transformation complete, Mother Mary then inquired if anyone else had a question. The next person was a woman who had been hospitalized with polio as a child and whose parents could not enter the room for much of her stay, as isolation was the protocol for polio in that time period. This early abandonment had caused her to feel unwelcomed, unloved, and was a pattern she had worked to change, but still found unbreakable.

Mother Mary had spoken before of what she called the "Original Wound," which occurred when our separation from Source was reinforced by our earthly curriculum in a traumatic way. Because we all felt like we had been torn away from unity and oneness, we searched for an answer why we would feel so alone and separate. The answer, however mistaken the interpretation, would often be that we were defective or bad because of rejection, either real or perceived experienced in early childhood.

For this woman, being left alone in a frightening, cold hospital environment without her twin sister or her parents, created a lifelong feeling of rejection and unworthiness.

Mother Mary suggested a remedy which could bring understanding to that frightened child. We moved the tables and chairs to create a makeshift hospital room and Frangelica chose several people from the group to play the roles of doctor, nurse, and of her family. We also chose someone to play Archangel Michael. Frangelica had always felt remarkably close to AA Michael, and that had brought her to Reno from Vermont to see if she could find more comfort and understanding in her life.

Earlier in my quest to understand human dynamics, I had trained in psychodrama and attended the world-renowned Moreno Institute in Beacon, New York, where I received my Directorship in Psychodrama. I had often used the skills I learned there to collaborate with individuals using other members of the group to play the parts needed to understand pivotal and traumatic events.

We began by taking Frangelica back to her childhood and being able to run and play before she became ill. Once she was in touch with that joyful sense of life, we moved into her illness and being taken to the hospital. The key in healing an event like this is not to pretend it never happened, but to bring comfort and a soul perspective into what otherwise would simply feel unfair and devastating.

The healing began when Frangelica could feel her original joy of being.

Then she chose someone else to be her lying in bed and I could question her as the wiser soul about what "good" could come of this. Frangelica also played the parts of her mother and father so I could ask them (being played by Frangelica) how they felt about their daughter being in the hospital. Both of her parents (expressed through Frangelica) spoke about their fear and frustration and how much they loved her.

The final part of the healing came when we put Frangelica back into the hospital bed and everyone, including AA Michael, stood by her, and sent Reiki and healing prayers and energy to her so her original fear and loneliness could be mitigated by this outpouring of love and the new understanding she had gained from seeing it through the eyes of her parents and her wiser self. Bathed in a sea of love from the group, from AA Michael and Mother Mary shifted her energy and created a new space for love and healing.

We ended the evening by standing in a circle, sharing a prayer for all of us and for all beings everywhere to feel love and to know they belong.

The next day, as I gave the keys to Ronna, she smiled at me and said, "I understand you did well last night." I felt embraced and understood by someone who had been doing what I was now doing for far longer, and was incredibly generous about sharing the spotlight and offering encouragement.

Repeatedly, I would learn, once you trust the still small voice, and follow where it leads, regardless of logic or convenience, miracles occur with increasing regularity. In May of 1999, three friends went with me to Sedona to the annual Madonna Ministers Conference. We loved this group and the chance to be in the beauty of Sedona to share our love and reverence for Mother Mary. As part of helping to raise funds, one friend's sister had designed a beautiful image of Mother Mary and we created dozens of bright blue sweatshirts emblazoned with "Madonna Ministry Sedona 1999." We each proudly wore ours and planned to sell the rest to raise money for the Madonna Ministry.

On the second day of the conference, I felt a sudden call to get out of the stuffy hotel conference room and be in the beauty of Sedona. It seemed so ironic we would have come to this beautiful place on the earth and be trapped inside a hotel conference room. I whispered to my three friends to see if they wanted to escape and "play hooky." When they nodded back, we left as quietly as we could, feeling like school kids on a snow day holiday!

Laughing with joy at our newfound freedom, we jumped in my car, not sure yet where we would head, happy to be outdoors and free to explore. As I pulled out of the hotel parking lot, it happened. It is a phenomenon I call "the tractor beam." Like the Star Trek crew, we were suddenly held and guided by a mysterious external force. Unlike the Star Trek episodes, this energy was benevolent and promised new delights.

We were guided up to Sedona's airport mesa, a popular ridge overlooking the town. At first, I thought we would stop at the renowned vortex where hikers feel the earth's energies. We pulled over and one of the other women said a beautiful prayer. The pull then was to continue into the parking lot of Sky Ranch, a picturesque motel with spectacular views. Still in the pull of the tractor beam, I drove to the farthest edge of the parking lot with the cliff drop off just inches away. Just as I was beginning to be concerned about the impending edge, the beam's hold released. We jumped out and looked around. We looked out at the view and down at the distant town, still puzzled about what we might find.

Slowly, my eyes moved upward to the bright blue sky dotted with puffy white clouds. A stillness and a palpable energy drew all of us to stare at a particular group of clouds. As we watched, the clouds shifted, and a perfect outline formed. It was Mother Mary. Her presence was unmistakable to all four of us. We could see her familiar image, arms stretching toward us, with six of the smaller clouds forming a crown of stars above her head. This was the exact depiction on the sweatshirts we had designed and two of us were wearing. Transfixed by her presence, we stood still as statues, humbled and awed.

Time stopped and as we opened to her love, Mother Mary offered each of us a transmission of light. We received not only the sight of her holy presence but also her blessing.

As the clouds shifted and the presence disappeared, we stood mesmerized by this treasured gift from our beloved Mother Mary. Not one of us had a camera. Still, her image lived in our hearts. There was a deep sense of having been touched and blessed by Mother Mary with a profound gift none of us would ever forget. As much as we later wanted to share our experience with friends and family, it somehow could not be translated. How do you share a gift so precious? What was next for each of us?

I wondered if Mary had a memory of her Discovery gateway. For Mary, it was the difficult journey to visit her cousin Elizabeth with both of them pregnant.

I had to go despite the danger and the difficulty. I thought at first it was to share my heart with my cousin, as indeed I did. And yet as I stood and Elizabeth touched my belly, she felt the child, who would be named John, quicken and leap inside her with some special joy. I knew then the meeting was of a far more profound nature. Jesus and John had to meet and allow their divinity and their physicality to form a profound connection. This power would bind them as brothers and strengthen each of them in the challenges of their separate journeys.

THE THIRD GATEWAY:
Committing to the Light
Solar Plexus Chakra
Sacrifice: Certainty
Gift: Passion

I am Creative

It is choice, not chance, which guides your life. In the center of your body is the power of your "gut" instinct. Let it lead you to new experiences and possibilities that feel joyful and uplifting.

Often people wonder about my name and where it came from. When asked if Samarah is my given name, I always smile and say, yes, it was given to me. As with so much, it was a gift from Mother Mary that built upon an earlier decision to follow my voice and knowing.

I had changed my first name from my birth name back in my early thirties. Born "Patricia," the other kids had called me "Patty" and despite being tiny, "Fatty Patty." That name always felt wrong and disparaging. Challenged by a workshop leader who suggested I take charge and change my name if it did not feel right; I was determined to have a name that felt like a match. I consulted with my best friend, John, after trying various forms of Patricia that still felt wrong. He always had better ideas. John was such a Renaissance Man. He was 6'4" with twinkling brown eyes that lit up any room he entered. He was my gentle giant. Like me, he was part of the residential staff working toward getting his Directorship in Psychodrama. He was also studying meditation, Buddhism and Bioenergetics so he could draw on a variety of modalities to help his clients.

We had become remarkably close, and I trusted his way of seeing things, as he always seemed to come from a place of love outside of the usual box. He suggested I was struggling too hard with names and focus instead on syllables. He also suggested that when I went to bed that night, I set the intention someone would call to me in the dream, and I would hear my name.

That night, as suggested, I put a pad and pen by my bed and set the intention I would hear my name in the dream. I will never forget the vibrant, full color dream I had. There, on a hillside in Greece, stood a white marble temple with beautiful columns. Standing alone at one end of the temple, I glimpsed a dozen young women in long white dresses, with headbands of gold standing at the other end. They were calling to me, and even in the dream, I strained to hear them. "Therah," they were calling, "Therah, come here."

I woke up, trembling with delight, went to find John and tell him about my dream. He smiled patiently as I excitedly shared what I had seen and heard. "Ah," he said, hearing Therah as two syllables: "Ra is the Egyptian sun god. I am glad you chose 'Rah' for the light inside you." Looking down with embarrassment at his praise, I felt the joy of renaming myself and being seen for who I am. From the first moment we met, John had looked into my heart and saw through any pretense or mask I wore.

Every moment with him was a gift and an opening. He looked through my disguises and saw me.

Since Therah seemed a bit too unusual, I took the name "Sarah" for my favorite grandmother and for its biblical nature. I used Sarah as my name for over twenty years, and even my parents and siblings finally gave in and addressed me as Sarah. As my work with Mother Mary became a greater and greater focus for me, she would often whisper things to me during the day to provide suggestions or comfort.

Happy to hear from her, I was confused when she kept insisting; I am inside you. I felt pleased and yet still not clear what she meant, I responded, "I know. You are inside all of us." She got a little exasperated by the second week of my saying this and so she showed me what she meant.

In my third eye vision appeared a little blue biplane, flying over a sandy beach with a banner streaming from its tail that said "Mary." Written in the sand beneath in lovely script was S A R A H. Just as the plane passed above the lettering, the MA from Mary dropped like a parachute bundle and fell into the middle of SARAH creating SA"MA"RAH.

As soon as I saw that; I understood what Mother Mary meant. I was to fully embrace her living presence inside me with my new name. I loved the sound of Samarah and the feeling of it and the meaning for me. So, on that day in 2000, I became Samarah. This is my true soul's name and the perfect fit for me. And, of course, when people ask me if Samarah is my given name, I smile and can truthfully say yes; my name was given to me by Mother Mary. To complete the commitment to my soul Path, I legally changed my name to Samarah Grace Daniels.

It was a proud moment for me, standing in front of the judge and affirming I was no longer Patricia, no longer Sarah, no longer my maiden name, no longer my married name. I was choosing how I would be known in the world for the rest of my life.

How difficult is it to choose Commitment to this Path with its elusive promise of soul freedom? In *The Dark Side of the Light Chasers*, Debbie Ford offers her candid assessment:

Unfortunately, most of us do not commit to what we really desire. We lie in bed at night and pray for a better life, a better body, a better job, but nothing changes. This is because we are lying to ourselves. What we pray for and what we have committed to are often different things. We pray for a healthy lifestyle but we are committed to being sedentary. We pray for a rewarding relationship but we are committed to sitting at home. We are most comfortable with the status quo (1998, p. 161).

In over two decades channeling Mother Mary and listening to the hundreds who have sought her counsel, I know Commitment is the most difficult gateway. In the early part of the Discovery process, we proudly brag about getting the best parking place or the serendipitous meeting of a friend because we felt guided to stop in a certain coffee shop.

Then, as the journey continues, we see where we are still captive to the criticism or praise of others or even to our own inner critic. We stay in the old patterns out of fear, or comfort, or simply because we believe if we wait long enough, we will not have to face what we do not want to see.

For Mother Mary, there were innumerable times she demonstrated her Commitment to the destiny she had chosen. From the first visit of Gabriel, she knew hers would not be an easy life and yet her faith and her courage, fortified by her inner knowing, said yes. I asked Mother Mary which of the earlier challenges she had faced required her deepest Commitment?

When Joseph and I traveled to Nazareth, I felt fear for the child within me. It was a difficult journey, and I wished so much for the comfort of my mother and my mid-wife. I knew we would not find comfort, only the charity of someone who pitied our plight. As the night wore on and the child was to be born, I cried out to Joseph. He held me and together we breathed as one so that our babe could be born. Despite my fears, there came such light as the child arrived that we could rejoice in that moment in that simple place for the honor and the blessing of what had occurred.

Mother Mary's commitment to Jesus and to the Path that was hers meant she would often have to set aside her own comfort and desires. She and Joseph raised Jesus and then allowed Jesus to go about his purpose, knowing the dangers he faced. She stood with Jesus and tended his body after the horror of the crucifixion. She fled with trusted followers to preserve the teachings and to keep alive the seeds that Jesus had planted of the new vision for humanity.

Even after her death, Mary's Commitment continues. In the messages and apparitions, Mary invites all who would live in love to take the steps that can lead to a new world. She reminds us that the tenets of love, compassion and equality offered by Jesus are the values which lead to peace and prosperity for all.

Offering remedies in places that have held destruction became part of the work Mary asked of me. Guided to be open and prayerful to whatever guidance I was given; I would be shown how to offer love. My first out-of-state trip was to Los Alamos, New Mexico. I invited a young friend to experience being guided by Spirit, and the magic it can bring. We flew into Albuquerque, rented a car, and headed out. We went first to Santa Fe and enjoyed the beauty and the vibrancy of this lovely town. Then we headed for Los Alamos, where the first nuclear bomb had been developed and where atomic research is still continuing. As we neared the town, she developed a splitting headache and asked if we could just turn around and head back to the more peaceful energies in Santa Fe.

I tuned in and asked for guidance and heard Archangel Gabriel say, "Sometimes you go to get and sometimes you go to give. You are here to give. Breathe in the peace of your deepest joy despite the energies you are sensing. All will be well." We followed the map to the Los Alamos research facilities, noting the signs along the fenced walls, "Danger--Do not stop". Led to a small grassy median area where there were several trees, I parked the car and nervously we got out. We were guided to build a small altar next to the largest tree, arranging the leaves and pinecones and stones in a symmetrical arrangement. Diane picked up her flute and played a beautiful song to the land and the trees that

held peace. I said a prayer, asking forgiveness and offering
blessings to all those who had been involved both in creating
the bomb and in suffering the consequences of its creation.
It was a deeply moving prayer for both of us. We felt the
spirits of those who had suffered, including the scientists and
researchers who had begun the work, believing it would be
a beneficial creation and then had to live with the results of
Hiroshima and Nagasaki. We reverently touched the ground
one last time, thanking the giant tree and the land and headed
back to the car.

Just as we got to the car, two security cars, lights
flashing, arrived, and boxed us in. I could only smile, as I
already knew what I was to say. "Oh officers, I am so glad
you are here. We were trying to find the highway and turned
the wrong way; can you help us?" They relaxed and directed
us where to turn and off we went, smiling at the serendipitous
timing and how we had been left alone just long enough to
complete the ceremony before the security patrol arrived.
It was an incredibly special trip and a reminder that when I
could follow the golden Path of light offered by the divine, all
would be overseen with ease and grace.

A deep awareness would come later, after we got back
to Arizona. I was born in 1945, the year the bombs were
dropped on Hiroshima and Nagasaki. I had not thought
about this trip as a karmic penance and yet it felt like part of
my history, the year I arrived had seen this atomic destruction
and anything I could do to amend such a devastating creation
would be welcome.

As we drove back toward Albuquerque, we stopped
at a diner for lunch. The server was especially friendly
and wanted to know where we had been and where we

were planning to stop. She mentioned an international school focused on peace and helping students from various backgrounds and ethnicities get along. She said, "You have to go see it!" Both of us had learned by now to pay close attention when someone said, "You HAVE to go there."

We felt we were being guided, and these casual remarks were part of our holy assignment. We got the directions and set out. We never found the school.

Instead, after driving the way we thought she had suggested and winding up on unpaved country roads in the middle of nowhere, we had nearly given up and were ready to turn around. It was then, in a farmer's field, just off the road, we saw it. It was a life-size statue of Mother Mary, along with a bench and lovely plantings surrounding it. This was not a tourist site. This was not even on a main road. There, in a farmer's field, Mother Mary had her special place. We got out, said a prayer, and laughed at the fact we had been following directions, thinking we were going to one place, and instead we find Mother Mary in the field. We felt blessed and reassured and simply knew the guiding hand of Mother Mary was with us as she is to anyone who seeks her.

Reassured by all the heavenly help, I planned my first pilgrimage overseas. Mary suggested I visit the sacred shrine dedicated to her in Lourdes, France. This is one of the holy sites where an apparition of Mary appeared to a young girl named Bernadette. My trustworthy friend who had gone to New Mexico with me signed up for the journey. We arrived in early November, knowing the crowds which filled this tiny town during the summer and early fall would not be there. Our flight landed in Paris, and we spent our first day enjoying the city and its sights. The next day we set out by train to the south of France. We were both quiet, not sure what to expect and somehow trying to understand what we might see. Were we there to witness a miracle or simply to walk in the footsteps of others who had?

Lourdes is set in the Pyrenees Mountains in the south of France. Over five million pilgrims visit this tiny town annually. In November, when we arrived, it was cold and still. Most of the storefronts and restaurants were boarded up for the winter. We made our way to the hotel and found a small cafe where we had a bowl of soup. There was a quiet presence in the town from so many religious travelers who had made the journey of faith. They had all come looking for something; to feel something. They all wanted to taste the grace of Mother Mary and to have their faith confirmed and experience the miracle of healing. Lourdes has been the site of thousands of healings, including over sixty miracles documented in a rigorous process overseen by the Catholic Church. All who come can breathe in the sanctity and the peace. Yet many who make the arduous journey, do not receive the healing they hoped to find.

The first night neither one of could sleep. About 10 pm we felt guided to take a walk, so we meandered through the deserted streets. We noticed an old fort on a hill that seemed to call to us as a destination. So, we walked, imagining we were there to bless and bring light to a place that had been built for war and defense. The rock face was sheer and shone with the lights from the fort and there was a great deal of moisture running down the rock and creating patterns.

We were both watching the play of light and water when we stopped in our tracks by the sense the water was forming into a palpable presence. Neither of us spoke. We watched, mesmerized, as the light and the water seemed to swirl and dance and come alive. As we watched, the head and shoulders of Mother Mary appeared, followed by her cloak, then her whole being was there, illuminated by the light above. She spoke to us.

Many come to Lourdes to find me. They look in the cathedral. They look in the grotto. They await me in the waters. Tell them I am everywhere. I appear when you listen. I appear when you hear the cries of the world. I appear when you are ready, and I appear when I am needed. There is no special place where you must go. There is no act of penance or tribute that I require. Tell them to open to the love that they believe they do not deserve. Tell them to see me, feel me, and know me as the love that resides in every heart. It is time to learn to love, not only to love another. Tell them they must love themselves. Without this, the world will continue to war, nation against nation, brother against brother, ideology against ideology. When the world is run by fear and domination, there is never enough to satisfy. It is soul hunger that must be fed. That requires love. This is the lesson that I am here to teach. Now go and sleep and dream of a world built on love, and live that dream, so it may come to life.

We made our way back to our room in silence and dreamed of a world built from love. I woke to the sounds of *Imagine* by John Lennon, as if he were serenading me in my dreams. With all my heart, I wanted to do whatever I could to create the world he and so many could only imagine.

That day, since the usual crowds were not there, we could experience the healing waters of Lourdes, in the stone baths the church had built. Escorted by the nuns into a tiny changing area, we were told to strip down to our underwear and wrap a sheet around us. It was already chilly as we shed our clothing and stood on the cold stone floor that November, in the Pyrenees. The water at Lourdes flows from a spring-fed stream that is ice cold. It is directed into concrete bathtubs, with a simple set of stairs at each end. Each tub is curtained off from the adjacent ones to offer a little privacy.

When it was my turn, two nuns stood on either side of me and escorted me into the tub area. They stood and gestured for me to take off the sheet and submerge myself. I laid the sheet on the side of the tub and went down three steps. The water was freezing. I went a little further and again they gestured to lie back in the water, and allow all of me to be submerged. I took a breath and did it, and without meaning to, as my body felt the icy jolt of the water, I exclaimed, "Yikes!" Later my friend, who was on the other side of the curtain, told me when she heard me yell, she looked at the nuns waiting with her and asked, "Cold?" to which they smiled and nodded an emphatic yes.

I walked out shivering and was ever so glad to put my clothes on, even though it was on top of my wet underwear. It was an experience only later I would feel into and notice how my heart felt clearer and happier. I felt so blessed I did not have any significant physical ills which needed attention. For me, the healing water, along with simply being in the energy of Bernadette and Mother Mary, allowed a freeing of my heart and a sense of immense gratitude for the blessings in my life.

Forewarned, my friend was prepared for the icy cold, and she shared later with me there had also been a sense of release and relief from being in those holy waters.

Later in the day, we were in the hotel lobby and noticed a woman in a wheelchair and her companion speaking to the desk clerk. My friend felt a powerful pull to the woman in the wheelchair and felt she was to sing for her. A gifted soul singer, my friend could sound the notes of each person's soul song, and hearing those notes often brought comfort and healing. She looked at the woman several times and then felt reluctant and too embarrassed to proceed.

Later, she asked me to bring in Mother Mary and channel a message to see what she could learn about this woman and what had happened.

Mother Mary said, This lady journeyed many miles to find healing. She hoped that Lourdes could bring her what she needed. You could have been her miracle. My friend felt the truth of this and was saddened, humbled by the knowledge she could have been an instrument of healing and had declined.

Both of us felt the impact of this experience, and we each looked back over our lives for the times we held back, not wanting to share what we felt guided to do, fearful of criticism or censure. I believe we both became even more determined to be courageous and not hold back the love and the gifts we could share

Later that evening, I felt Mother Mary offering insights into the necessity for courage and also into why we had come to this remote village. These are the words Mother Mary offered at Lourdes.

Be Not Afraid

I have come to remind you of who you are and why you have come. "Be not afraid" is what Gabriel said to me, a young girl unsure of what my life would bring. "Be not afraid," he said as he came to offer me a glimpse of my part in the story of humanity's journey to love.

"Be not afraid," I say to you as I ask of you to see your part in what is to come. "Be not afraid" as you hear my voice and the inner guidance of your angels and teachers. "Be not afraid" that this is some kind of madness." Be not afraid" that you will lose what you have so carefully worked to gain. "Be not afraid" for this is the time and the promise that you have come to fulfill.

Each birth is a miracle. It is the joining of humanity and divinity. It is the creation of life that offers so much promise and possibility. Each of you has a destiny, and yet it is not without choice.

When I first came to Bernadette in the small village in France, my first words to her were "be not afraid." She did not know who I was and yet, in her innocence and love, she could receive and trust the message that I offered. At first, the learned priest did not believe her, for he associated me with grandeur and pomp. That was never what I lived. The true glory of life is in innocence and devotion to love.

Bernadette was not afraid. She continued to tell what she heard and offer what was given to her. All of you are given this same chance each day. Will you tell what you know, or will you be silent in the face of authority? Will you share a vision of a brighter world that has been offered to you or will you be silent and submit to the prison of judgment and self-censure?

I ask of each of you to be not afraid of the guidance that you receive that fills your heart with hope and your being with love. See what you see and tell what you know. This world now totters on the brink of dissolution from the degradation of life and earth's resources and the careless disregard that has been permitted.

You are all now the carriers of the seeds of the New Earth. All of you must be the gardeners that plant and tend what you would harvest in the coming days. If you want peace, you must plant the seeds of justice for all. There can be no peace as long as there are people living without shelter, food, and water.

How will you have a thriving planet if the air and water and earth are so degraded that they no longer nourish you? Here too, be not afraid. It is time to understand and work with the forces of nature and Gaia in a partnership of co-creation. Where soil is depleted, it must now be restored. Where deforestation has created erosion and devastation, it is time to plant and rejoice as the renewal springs forth.

You each have a part to play. Be not afraid. Listen to what is whispered to you from the voices of light. Then, be a part of all the good that can now become the legacy of light that you and so many others choose to live.

Each time that I have come as a visitation and those who saw me told the story, a holy place was made. I tell you now; the whole earth is holy as are all of the galaxies. It is time to be a part of that consecration. Be not afraid. I am here with you, to remind you that you, too, are a child of God in a body of light made manifest on earth that you might taste of your glory as you heal your belief in aloneness.

Be Not Afraid. It is time and I am with you.

We sat there in the tiny room in Lourdes, knowing thousands of pilgrims had come and thousands more would come, looking for healing and peace. In that quiet, we both promised we would no longer be afraid to share our light as we were guided. There was great comfort in that commitment and yet, as with all commitments, more challenges would come for each of us.

The sacrifice our Commitment requires is the sacrifice of *Certainty*. The profound gift we receive is *Faith*. We will need every ounce of faith for the next gateway where we encounter Tribulation.

THE FOURTH GATEWAY:
Tested by the Light
Heart Chakra
Sacrifice: Comfort
The Gift: Compassion

I Am Loving

No one is ever lost to God, simply for a moment to themselves. Their light and their vision become obscured by fear, doubt, prejudice, greed, and anger. The violence in your world is a desperate attempt to get back home to the light, and the wrongly held belief that it is your brother who keeps you from that which you seek.

Despite the blessings and joy of following the Path, into every spiritual life will come a time of Tribulation, the biblical dark night of the soul. We fall to our knees from the pain and difficulty of an illness, or loss, or challenge. We question our Path and cry out to God about the unfairness of our suffering. We beseech Him to intervene, and we feel betrayed by God because we had been trying so hard to do His will.

Andrew Harvey, one of my favorite teachers and a lover of Mary, reminds us of the struggle and the importance of keeping our hearts open even as we suffer betrayal and condemnation.

We need at every single level of our evolution to be able to keep alive the heart of the divine child, the heart that longs and loves and gives and is always ready for new struggle and new revelation, always ready for another vast death and vast rebirth. This is Jesus' tremendous instruction to us about the core consciousness that can baptize us in the glory of the living Christ. We see in his own example of great vulnerability and tenderness and infinite flexibility and constant love and support of others, we see this glorious, tender, childlike quality erupting through his gravity and through the horror of what he suffered repeatedly and again as a sign of the ecstatic freedom that lived in him as his deepest secret and his deepest gift to those who love him and follow him in this Path (Harvey, 2013).

Even Jesus, as he is crucified, calls out to God to save him from his horrific torment. And yet, on this Path to find our way, it is often at the darkest moment we find a place inside us that wills us to survive and to consecrate this challenge and transform it into grace.

For Mary, standing by the cross as her son suffers this most horrific of deaths, she, too, may have questioned how this could be God's will and how this could ever shift from a sacrifice into a sacrament. I asked her to describe how this felt to her as she endured the Gateway of Tribulation.

Any of you that have lost a child, there is no solace, no comfort for that heartache. My mind knew that this, too, was part of God's holy plan, and yet I could not help but question why it must be thus. Every part of me ached with his pain. My heart wept with his. I did not speak aloud and yet my voice was with his when he cried out to Father for release. I fell to my knees and was again as a helpless child

Peter carried me away from the sight of my son's suffering and yet my sorrow did not abate.

One of my darkest times came when I first shared with my long-time spiritual group, I was channeling Mother Mary. We had met together and meditated and prayed together for years, and I considered each of them a treasured friend. One woman I was especially close to had asked me to support her while her husband was dying of lung cancer. She begged me to rent a place close to her so she could rely on my comfort in this most difficult of times. I agreed and stayed near her for the six months until he passed.

It was this same woman who would reject me when I shared my excitement about the visitations from Mary and the request to be her messenger. When I had excitedly shared my news, she looked at me with disbelief and, curling her mouth with disdain, sarcastically said, "Aren't you special?" When I did not rise to the bait, she whispered to the others in the group, saying my ego had taken over and I was no longer fit to lead the meditations, and should be asked to leave.

Hurt and puzzled, I confronted her about spreading these rumors. She donned a false look of concern and suggested, "I think you are having a psychotic break and should seek treatment." Feeling uncertain and betrayed, I called my Reiki Master, who had also been this woman's teacher, and asked for her counsel. I knew my Reiki Master would not take sides, and I hoped she could provide insight into what this was and why it was happening.

I poured out my heart to her and waited. Her piercing blue eyes bored into mine with clarity and strength as she offered, "It really is quite simple. This is a test of what you believe. If you believe it is Mother Mary and you are to follow this Path, then what others say about it should not deter you." I felt the honesty of this and although it hurt to lose these friendships, I knew mine was another road.

Once I left the group and made a heartfelt Commitment to the life I had chosen with Mary, I no longer worried if there were people who did not believe me or who wanted to label me as crazy. I stepped back from the world's view of me and entered the Path of grace I felt as I opened increasingly to Mary. It is not for the faint of heart.

When I doubted or felt lonely, I took comfort in reading the accounts of the visionaries who saw Mary at Fatima, Lourdes and Medjugorje. All shared one common experience. All of them were doubted, ridiculed, and teased, as I had been. Despite the reception they received from family and community, all of them made a Commitment to what they had seen and believed to be Mother Mary.

Bernadette was a young girl of fourteen on February 11, 1858, when she first saw Mary at what would become the shrine of Lourdes. When she shared the story with her mother and sister, her mother spanked them both for "such nonsense" (Odell, 2010, p. 98). Days later, despite being punished for her insolence, Bernadette was again drawn back to the grotto with a few of the town's children. She again saw Mary and was drawn into a kind of trance.

Worried for her safety in the rocky grotto, one man from town carried her back, as she had become rigid and unmoving. Bernadette's mother, angered at what she considered her daughter's antics, approached her with a stick.

The next day, at the Abbey, one of the Sisters slapped Bernadette and forbid her to return to the grotto. Nonetheless, Bernadette, at the request of two of the influential ladies of the town, did go back. Again, she dropped to her knees and fell into a trance. This time, Mother Mary asked her to return for fifteen days in a row and Bernadette agreed.

Still, there was little support for Bernadette. The outraged Police Commissioner got involved and brought Bernadette in for questioning. He threatened her for what he believed were crimes against the church. The disputes and threats continued and yet Bernadette felt Mary's call so strongly, despite the opposition of her family and the Police, she kept going.

On the day Mary told Bernadette to scrape away at the dirt by the grotto, and then drink the water she found, Bernadette horrified the crowd by drinking what looked like mud. Murmuring she had gone mad; the crowd grew restless and doubtful. When the crowd returned just days later, the spring of Lourdes was running at an amazing rate.

Bernadette's vigil continued to attract larger and larger gatherings. On March 1, Mother Mary gave her the message to tell the priest a chapel must be built at the grotto where people could come in procession.

It would be years before the chapel was built, and yet because of Bernadette's unflagging Commitment and the faith of those who came, it is now the most well-known of the Marian sites with visitors numbering in the millions each year. Bernadette became a nun at the Convent in Nevers and worked tirelessly in the infirmary until her health failed her.

"On April 16, 1879, Easter Wednesday, the little sister who had seen the Mother of the Lord breathed her last. She was thirty-five years old. Her body, marvelously preserved from any corruption, lies in state to this day in the convent chapel at Nevers" (Odell, 2010, p.112).

Another visionary who endured personal Tribulation and suffering was a young woman in Rwanda, who had her first visitation in 1981 (Odell, p. 239). Alphonsine Mumureke was just sixteen and working at a Catholic boarding school in the dining room when she heard a voice calling "my daughter." When she followed the voice to another room, she heard Mother Mary and had a conversation so powerful, she fell to the floor in a kind of trance when it was over. Her story about what happened, that she excitedly shared once she came back from the trance, was not believed. She was teased and ridiculed for making up ridiculous stories to get attention.

To rectify the injustice, Mother Mary appeared to first one other girl and then four more. Soon, pilgrims were coming from every region to witness the transmissions. On the eighth anniversary of the first visitation, Alphonsine saw Mary for the last time. Over 10,000 people attended that day. Alphonsine's strong Commitment and willingness to endure Tribulation allowed those dwelling in hardship and poverty to find faith again.

It is hard to endure the censure often encountered by those who receive and then share a mystical experience. Yet, for those courageous enough to stand in their knowing and trust the truth they have witnessed, the hunger others have to feel connected to God, may inspire them first out of curiosity and then perhaps from faith to seek beyond the known for a connection to God.

Discernment in the times of tribulation will help us choose the way out or through the challenges we face. Alana Fairchild, in one of her channeled books, *Crystal Masters 333* offers this advice: "Sometimes, our discernment might tell us that retreat is a wise course of action. The discernment in that situation is to know when to cut your losses and step back in the face of a larger foe you are unprepared to successfully confront" (2014, p. 219).

Each time of tribulation assesses our commitment to the way of love. What keeps me steady are the miraculous moments when I can help free someone from the grip of fear and conditioning. Mother Mary's loving touch created a miracle for a young woman named Serena. Serena had first come to my monthly prayer group with another friend from Unity Church. Serena was silent; she seemed frightened and uncomfortable about being with a group. She lived alone and had never learned to drive, so she felt isolated, lonely. It seemed like she wanted to change, and yet how could she trust "strangers"?

I invited her to my next Dare to Dream weekend retreat. I doubted she would come, as she was so reluctant and uncomfortable with sharing anything about herself. To her credit, and really also to the urging of her friend, she came. For the first day, she hung back and did not take part. Still, she stayed.

Day two, as we went around the group to share our stories, it was Serena's turn. I asked her, "What do you think it would take for you to feel safe enough to share with us?" Startled by this question, she looked down at her lap, avoiding eye contact. I waited. We all waited and sent love. Finally, Serena looked up and said, "I need to break my mother's hold on me. She always put me down and made me feel small and stupid." I asked her what action she could take that would demonstrate an end to her mother's grip. "I need to smash this dragon necklace she gave me." Without missing a beat, I stood up and said, "Let's go!"

We gathered outside. I found a huge rock she could use to put the necklace on, and someone brought a hammer from the shed. I wrapped the necklace in a cloth so the shards could not fly off and hurt anyone. We gathered together, held hands and the group affirmed we all stood with Serena in her decision to take back her power and have freedom for herself and her life. Guided by Mother Mary, I suggested Serena say aloud whatever she felt. In the strongest voice I had ever heard from her, she bellowed, "Get out! I am done!"

Again, feeling the gentle urging of Mary, I suggested she say it three times, getting louder each time, and on the third one, smash the necklace. The group stepped back to give her room, while still holding her with love. With all her strength and courage, Serena shouted those words and the third time, smashed the necklace with all her might. When we opened the cloth, the necklace was in pieces. I asked Serena what she wanted to do with it, and she wanted to bury it. We found a little spot in the woods where she dug a grave to bury any remnant of being a victim. She offered one more prayer to end the feeling of being a prisoner. Now she could open to new beginnings. She was free!

For the rest of the weekend, Serena was quiet and yet very much with us. I saw her talking with the group during the breaks and laughing with the others in the kitchen. I was truly glad for her, and yet I did not know what miracles were yet to come in her new life of freedom.

About a month later, Serena called to tell me she was dating someone. I was astonished as until this weekend, she had rarely left her house and had to take the bus wherever she went since she did not drive. Matt soon became her steady boyfriend, and they shared a love of animals, computers and quiet. They left Arizona and moved to Oregon to have more room for their family of animals. I asked her to stay in touch and felt so blessed I had been part of her emergence from such a solitary life.

The next year, Serena called me again and asked me if I would officiate their wedding in Oregon. I flew to Portland, where they had organized one of the sweetest private ceremonies I had ever seen. They had made their own wedding apparel and decorations and the wedding was in the beautifully decorated back yard of their friend's home.

Serena and Matt wanted to walk down the aisle together and they walked barefooted to show their love of the earth and their commitment to a simple, sacred life. They had written their own vows and the tenderness and sweetness between them still brings tears to my eyes. What a blessing to see how her life had changed. She is now happily married, surrounded by friends and her beloved animals, and living a life she loves. Her courage, along with the support she felt, allowed her to break a lifelong pattern of suffering and create a new way of being in the world.

Global tribulation arrived on September 11, 2001, when the hijackers shattered any sense of safety about living in America. Much of the world began a war on terror that is still raging. My plans for a Peace Pilgrimage to Medjugorje, in Bosnia, with a group led by Jimmy Twyman scheduled for 9/13/2001, were also shattered as all flights were cancelled. I was scheduled to go with a dear friend and fellow Madonna Minister. On 9/11/2001, when the planes hit the World Trade Center along with the crashes in Pennsylvania and the Pentagon, everything changed. So many dreams and desires for peace seemed to go up in smoke along with the towers collapsing. All were in shock.

How could this happen when so many had been praying and working for peace? What could we do now as the world mourned and the desire for retribution led to the troop's deployment? How would we ever know peace?

Like everyone who felt the depth of the horror and loss of 9/11, I wanted to do something, to offer my love. I decided to record a message from Mother Mary and create a CD. I felt Mother Mary could offer us some kind of explanation or comfort about 9/11, since I felt derailed and overwhelmed by the devastation. I located a wonderful sound man who had a recording studio attached to his home, hired an artist to design the cover and looked into the costs of duplication and packaging.

On October 11, 2001, exactly one month after 9/11, I recorded a message from Mother Mary about the attacks called, "The Awakening." She challenged us to see this horrific experience as an opportunity for new possibilities. We could see it as a time to step up and create the world we wanted, not retaliate with the same brutality shown to us. In part, what she offered was:

Here on your earth, there is such promise, such possibilities. It is time to ask yourselves, what is my part in creating this new world? There was also one admonition:

If it is to be written in fear, it is your fear that will create it. If it is to be written in love, it is your love that will create it.

The message from Mother Mary was clear to me. Each of us has the choice of how much we will extend ourselves into the world. How much will we risk? How far out of our comfort zone might we travel to create new Pathways? I mailed my CD with a Christmas card to everyone I had met through Mother Mary and offered to come to their town and bring Messages from Mother Mary. I sent out one hundred cards and CDs and waited to see what might unfold.

From the one hundred I had sent out, I got just one response. The call came from Frangelica, the woman I had met in Reno at the Archangel Michael weekend workshop. She had attended the evening channeling I had done and received a healing around her early childhood polio experience. She was living in a small town in Vermont but said she would do her best to promote an "Evening with Mother Mary" talk, and a few private sessions. I said yes. I had said to Mother Mary I would go where invited and speak to those who would listen. Frangelica asked if I needed a certain amount of money guaranteed before I could commit. I said no, I would come and trust all would be as Mary wished it to be. Since Frangelica would be doing all the work and providing me a place to stay, we agreed to share any of the money collected 50/50.

I did ask if she knew of anyone else in New England who might be interested in hosting me. Here is where things got even more interesting.

One of the many heartbreaks in my life had been making a series of decisions which led to being out of work, out of money, and out of luck. This led me to contact my son's father and ask for financial support. Instead, he asked if my son could live with him for a while until I landed another job. When I asked my nine-year-old how he felt about the idea, he said, "You mean he really does love me like you always said?" His father had remarried, and the new wife did not want any contact with me and therefore, had forbidden his father to have anything to do with his son; so, he had not seen or talked to my son in six years.

I went back to the phone and planned for Michael's flight. When I went back to see how my son was doing, he had taken his Cub Scout uniform out of the closet. "Mom," he said, "I want to wear my uniform. Then, you can tell dad what I will be wearing, because he doesn't know what I look like anymore." In that one sentence from my nine-year-old, there was so much wisdom and so much heartbreak.

Weary of the fruitless job hunt in Boulder, I returned to NY and stayed at my mother's for a few weeks and quickly found a job, this time in Flemington, NJ, teaching high school English. I called my son's father with the news, ready to plan to pick up my son and start my new job. That was not what happened.

Back in New York at my mom's house, we were having a quiet dinner and my plan was to leave the next day to drive to NH and pick up my son. There was a knock at the door, and it was a uniformed police officer. He handed me a summons. Stunned and not sure what this could be, I opened it to find out my ex-husband was suing me for custody, saying I had "abandoned" my son.

Reeling from this betrayal, I sat down to collect myself and shared the news with my mother and brother. Expecting sympathy and support, I was stricken when my mother said, "Maybe it's for the best, as this way he will have a mother, father, sister, and brother." I got up from the table and walked out the door, knowing anything I said at that point would be from hurt and anger.

The next few years were incredibly challenging. Child custody suits are heard in the state where the child is living. Thus, each time I wanted to go to court, I had to drive from New Jersey to New Hampshire and take time off from work, since the court meets during the week. In addition, my son was told I had begged them to take him off my hands and I was not interested in providing a home for him. Each time I would make plans for visitation, his father would have "forgotten" it was my weekend, and no one would be home. I could not reach my attorney on the weekend, so I would simply have to drive back to New Jersey, frustrated, heart sick and feeling helpless.

I dislike feeling helpless. Despite the lack of support from my family, I knew I had to do something that would let my son know I had never abandoned him, and what he was being told was not true. Left to my own heart, I sat down and meditated, and asked I be guided to a solution for the highest good of all of us. Days later, I saw a job opening for a high school English teacher in New Hampshire in the town next to where my son was living with his father. I applied immediately, got the job, arranged the move, heartened by this sign, and feeling like I had regained a measure of my confidence.

As soon as I was settled, I called them and said I was now living nearby and planned to see my son every weekend.

Stunned silence greeted me and I knew pitched battles lay ahead. Once I lived close by, they could no longer avoid me. Angered by this development, my ex husband's wife began to treat my son poorly. She would get lavish presents for her two children and something far less for my son. She would criticize him if he asked for extra helpings of food, saying he was already chunky enough.

We had shouting matches and angry exchanges. I had turned to real estate, since my teaching job in that small town offered one of the lowest salaries in the region. There were teachers working full time who still qualified for food stamps because of low pay.

While living in New Hampshire, I had endured a long series of emotional and financial challenges. It ended when my son came back to live with me, having discovered the truth of what had happened and fed up with his stepmother's cruelty. Her last act was to go through the family photo album and cut my son's face out of every photo and hand him an envelope with all the scraps of what might have been happy times. Her comment was, "Now you are no longer in our family."

Reunited, my son and I had happy years there while he finished high school. I was hopeful he would go to college, but he opted to join the navy. Once he left for his six-year enlistment, I could not wait to get out of there. I sold the house, moved to Arizona stating loudly and emphatically to anyone who would listen, "I am NEVER returning to New Hampshire."

Now that I have gotten clarity about how the universe works, I have found anytime I want to say "never"; I may as well open my arms and say, "Bring it on!" Every experience or feeling we try to push away or ignore stays in the shadow and keeps us from true peace and authenticity.

Without knowing how much of the time I lived in New Hampshire was still in a dark place in my heart, I soon learned part of the healing Mother Mary was engineering would be to create a time in New Hampshire that was joyous, welcoming, and fulfilling.

Frangelica had called her friend Jenny in New Hampshire to ask if she would sponsor me. Jenny asked when and Frangelica indicated I would be coming May 2002. "Oh no," Jenny said, "I have several birthdays and Mother's Day." Suddenly, Jenny paused and said, "Wait, incoming message". She, too, could hear Mother Mary and felt the urgency of this timing, and said, "OK, that will be fine." Jenny even agreed to pick me up at the Manchester, New Hampshire airport, as it would be most convenient, and I could do a Mother Mary Evening at her house.

Frangelica would drive down and bring me to Vermont. I was still healing my early disappointment, trusting all would work out without worrying about every little detail. Mother Mary has such a sense of humor about the lessons she offers, and each one seems to come wrapped in a special gift basket with a name I will not forget. Thus, one day, she told me I needed to "mind my P's and Q's." For those of you who have not heard that expression, it is used as a reminder often from parents or teachers to mind your manners. Mother Mary explained it in a unique way.

Your manner is how you look at your life and your way of being and the choices that you are offered.

The manners that I wish you to mind are your P's and Q's. The P's that matter Power, Passion, Presence, Purpose, Promise, Path and Possibility. These are the gauges of how you are living your life.

The Q's that matter are the following Questions, "Is it loving? Is it for my highest good? Does it serve me and the world? What will be the cost to my heart or the heart of another? Do I feel more alive if I choose this? Is it mine to do or to offer, or is it the Path for another? Will this contribute to the legacy of light that I would like to leave behind?

If you mind those seven P's and allow each of those seven Q's to be part of your inner dialogue, you will find that your life begins to follow a Path of light and ease.

I know as I let go of the mental traps of trying to figure everything out and just surrender to what feels right and expansive rather than dark and limiting, doors open, and my heart continues to heal. I believe, besides the damage done when someone betrays or hurts us, the damage is made even greater and more enduring by what we tell ourselves about it. "It was my fault." "If I had been prettier, sexier, or richer, this would not have occurred." We layer on guilt, shame, or regret and lose confidence in our ability to make better choices. Once I accepted the new formula for minding my P's and Q's, I shifted the focus of power to my inner knowing and was no longer dependent on outside reinforcement or approval.

Thus, I returned to New Hampshire, welcomed, and embraced by loving friends and the beauty of the spring flowers. In May we had rain, sun, and snow because in Arizona

I kept complaining about missing the seasons. Jenny took a fantastic picture of me making snowballs on her back deck in May!

Following the guidelines to choose from love and the Ps and Qs altered everything about my life. Along with prayer and meditation, I opened to seeing myself as a chalice of light and goodness. I could keep full by staying attuned to my higher self and being extremely conscious of the choices I made. I stopped using a linear way of assessing plans and saw everything as energy I could move toward or away from, and could also command with my intention and openness.

Another way of describing this shift would be I operated as a spiritual being having a physical experience, so my reference points for meaning became how much light and love I felt.

We can derive inspiration and comfort from true stories of Commitment and Tribulation that show how, if we will stay the course, there can be a time of justice and Rebirth. Nelson Mandela, the hero of the African people imprisoned for years, and finally released, became the leader of the nation. He, along with other great heroes like Aung San Suu Kyi of Myanmar, Martin Luther King Jr., and Mahatma Gandhi, endured years of tribulation and yet did not falter in their commitments to the truths they held. A contemporary hero and winner of the Nobel Peace Prize is Malala Yousafzai of Pakistan. Shot by the Taliban and left to die, she not only lived, but is now a global spokesperson for the rights of girls. These are inspirational modern stories of Commitment, Tribulation and how with persistence and courage we can arrive at the next Gateway: Rebirth.

THE FIFTH GATEWAY:
Rebirth of Light
Throat Chakra
The Sacrifice: Belonging
The Gift: Authenticity

I Am Worthy

Look up and see the Light that has never left you. As you dwell in the presence of this truth, you are Home. This is love, bringing light fully into the body, heart, and mind, consecrating the light, cherishing the light, allowing the light. Then every expression is one of love, for there is only love to offer.

When Jesus rose from his tomb after three days, his re-birth allowed him to become a lasting presence that continues to invite humanity to find a Path to love. When Mother Mary had to leave her homeland and go into hiding with a small group of the devoted, did she also create some kind of rebirth? I asked Mother Mary to describe her Rebirth after the pain of Tribulation.

The wonder and the sweet joy of feeling my son again, even through the veil of death, gave me courage and a respite from my mourning. His reassurance that his spirit would always attend me, even as he dealt with the world, allowed me to trust that I could leave our home and travel to a new land. Indeed, I thought I might simply live as an old woman, not the mother of the Savior, and I longed for the simplicity such a life might offer. And so, we set out to a new land and a new life.

Over the centuries since her death, Mother Mary's presence has continued to offer love, inspiration, and comfort to millions of Christians and non-Christians alike. The transition from being the Mother of the Savior to becoming the Mother of All is a testament to how powerfully the pain of tribulation can be consecrated into the holy fire of Rebirth.

In the last two sessions of the online Christ Path course, Andrew Harvey explored what might be possible if these are indeed the times when the Divine Human is being fully birthed. As Andrew described it:
"It is an alchemical process that we are in, a process of transfiguration, a process of being reborn into and as love, eternal love in a body in action, the transcendence embodied."

That is what we know now on our journey, the Christ Path, through the years. It is a Path of total abandon in a love beyond reason but infused by Divine Peace and consciousness of Divine Identity embracing all opposites in the mystery of persons.

We know that the essence of the Christ Path is the transfiguration process. We know too that the essence of the transfiguration process is the birthing of a new world, a world irradiated by love in all its intimate selves and particles and quarks and neutrinos. For this transfiguring process to work there has to be a death, a crucifixion by love and by the pain of the shadow of the full self, the death of the full self (2013).

My Rebirth required I bring to light my hidden shadow

and heal the pain of my earlier years. I went to Debbie Ford's Shadow workshop. Ford had pioneered this work after healing from her earlier self-destructive Path of bulimia and drugs. Her New York Times bestselling book, *The Dark Side of the Light Chasers* (1998), chronicles how people avoid pain and discomfort by masking their emotions or drowning them. In the process, innocence is lost, as well as any connection with sacredness.

In the deepest, most challenging part of the workshop, participants are blindfolded, and required to shout out their deepest fears about themselves. Ford believed we cannot be free until we claim all of our qualities. I had no problem saying I was greedy and selfish and a few other not so desirable qualities. Where I was stuck was on the "golden shadow" aspects, qualities like glorious, beautiful, precious, and loveable.

The facilitator asked me to take off the blindfold and look into her eyes and one by one say each of them. "I am glorious, I am beautiful, I am precious, and I am loveable." At first, I whispered them, looking away and down each time, embarrassed and uncomfortable. Repeatedly, she urged me to accept each one. My voice got louder and louder until I was shouting the words. As the tears fell with both relief and recognition, she grabbed me by both arms, looked deeply into my eyes, and proclaimed with great tenderness, "You are glorious, you are beautiful, you are precious, and you are loveable."

Something broke free within me, and as I started to sob, she held me gently against her. I looked up again at her and we both laughed and danced, and chanted my new song, "I am glorious, I am beautiful, I am precious, and I am loveable." From that weekend on, I felt free and reborn.

The miracles of Mother Mary have brought Rebirth to those who find their way to her. Arthur Boyle first went to Medjugorje in 2000, when he had been given only months to live because of the cancer which had invaded his body. He had given up and was preparing to die when two friends convinced him to make the trip. He said his confession the first night and felt an immense relief. The next morning, he met with one visionary and asked for her help. She held his hand and petitioned Mother Mary as Arthur's two friends joined in the prayer. Boyle felt a heat pour through his body. Once he had returned to Boston, he had a new CT scan revealing his tumors had nearly disappeared.

Since the first trip, he has returned thirteen times. He shares he knew he had to change his life and now is a devout believer in the power of "the Mother and her intercession" (Orth, *National Geographic*, p. 36).

My confidence in my soul Path, along with a deeper faith in my channeling, grew as I trusted and allowed. In 2007, when I met Andrew Harvey in Chicago and took part in his weekend training in Spiritual Activism, I offered to do a Mother Mary channeling for the group, and he agreed. When Mother Mary had delivered her message, she asked if anyone wanted to ask a question and Andrew's was the only hand raised. He asked of Mother Mary, "Is the birth (of the New Earth) inevitable?"

Mother Mary's answer was:
No, it is up to each and every one of you to awaken and do your part; thus, the awakening lies within your hands.

Later, Andrew came over to thank me for the channeling and said something deeply affirming, "I know you are channeling Mary's love. It truly is up to each of us. Had you answered that the birth was inevitable, regardless of our actions, I would have known you were not channeling Mary. Thank you for being her messenger with such integrity."

During the *Christ Path* course, Andrew Harvey suggested two great births took place in Jesus' own life and example. In the first birth that took place in the stable, there was an "eruption into a dimension of a new Father-Mother consciousness that was going to unite the deepest revelations in an evolutionary passion" (2013).

The second birth, the resurrection, was a Rebirth and "a vast nuclear explosion of divine love and triumph" (2013). Harvey then affirmed, "when you bring these two births together, then what they're opening up for us is a birth that will bring us to a wholly new level of embodied divinity."

Our rebirth is really a remembering of a state of grace we hold within us. Mother Mary reminds us it is time to find our way back by following the Path of light we are offered. We have now received the gift of Trust by sacrificing the limiting tribal demands of Belonging. This new depth of Trust will lead us to the next Gateway, the Gateway of Knowing.

One of the life-changing miracles of Rebirth I witnessed began with a dire prediction by Mother Mary. This individual would have to open the gateways of Awakening and Discovery and make a Commitment to a series of drastic life changes. Melody was one of the earliest of those who came to receive a private message from Mother Mary. Usually, Mother Mary's messages were gentle. She would listen to the questions and/or concerns of the individual and then quietly suggest ways that might help them feel more love or have more peace and joy.

Mother Mary did not offer psychic predictions. She did indicate how the current choices someone was making would have outcomes. For Melody, the message was powerful, direct, and foreboding. A hardworking young woman struggling with diabetes and supporting both her ill mother and her often out-of-work sister, Melody rarely complained. She believed she was supposed to support her family because that was how to show love. Mother Mary listened to Melody pour out her frustration and concern. I reached out and took her hand. Staring directly into Melody's eyes, Mother Mary said,

If you continue this way of living, you will be dead in a year.

Stunned by this direct and powerful message, Melody's journey over the next ten years illustrates the sacrifices and the gifts of the journey through the seven gateways. Her courage in Awakening, Discovering, and learning to trust allowed her to risk and endure the savage rejection of her family. She had to open to the new and Surrender to the Knowing she was meant to have a joyous life.

For Melody, the courage to find her way and to endure the censure of her birth family was driven by her inner knowing that what Mother Mary had told her was the voice of true, unconditional love. That was the Path she was determined to follow.

The sacrifice at this gateway is belonging. Melody had to leave her sister and mother and endure loneliness for a time. She quit one of her three jobs and went back to school to create more opportunity for a career. She joined a new church and trained to be a chaplain. Now she serves with gratitude and deep love, surrounded by her new loving family and the life partner she has now wed. In Melody's own words, "As I look around my life now, I have a beautiful new family who love and accept me. I have eleven grandchildren to light up my life. I have a wonderful job. I completed first a Master's, and then a doctorate; all because I chose life, my life. I have grown more in these years since I chose life than in all my previous time on earth."

For much of my life, I have felt like an outsider. I kept feeling there was another place, another time where I belonged. I did not trust the experts, counselors and teachers, famous people who promised fame and fortune. It was as if I could feel their disparity. I heard their words, but I did not feel authenticity. It was if everyone was simply playing a part, waiting to cast me in their play.

My mother was dying. As I sat by her bed each day at the inpatient hospice facility, I tried to find ways to reconnect with her. Her mind was still sharp. Her body was weary and wracked with pain until the morphine drip did its work. I brought her favorite magazines and read to her or played music.

One day I asked what she remembered about me as a kid. I was hungry for a story that might be a memory I could hold on to after she was gone. She struggled a moment, and then with an undisguised accusatory look of disappointment, she said, "You always had to go your own way."

It was not the story I wanted to hear. It made neither of us smile or bring us closer. Still, once I had a chance to reflect on her accusation, I realized it was true. After her death, I could remember that moment and smile. It was a testimonial to my authentic self. From my earliest days, I had listened and been guided by this inner authority.

I still struggled with achievement. What was it I wanted to achieve?

Raised on fairy tales of happily ever after; what did it mean that I was single? In a world where money is the most common measure of success, what did it mean that I was not on some fast track to millions? I found solace in the Madonna Ministry, a worldwide church without walls, dedicated to the feminine spirit of compassion and service. I offered to channel a message from Mary at our annual gathering in Phoenix. What came through that day inspires me still.

As I stood to offer the message, the energy was so powerful I asked a friend to hold my feet so I would not faint. The room grew quiet. I closed my eyes, and the voice of Mary rang out:

There are no lesser lights! Each of you has a part to play. Align with what brings you the greatest joy and peace. Fill yourself to overflowing. Thus, you are not a cauldron full of fear and doubt. You become a cup, filled with light. Soon it overflows and you are the chalice. Whether you are baking cookies or building orphanages, you are the hands and heart of my love. Rejoice in that happy truth.

The priceless gift of authenticity that comes with Rebirth opens us even further to our Knowing, the next gateway.

THE SIXTH GATEWAY:
Knowing the Light
Third Eye Chakra
The Sacrifice: Approval
The Gift: Peace

I Am Compassionate

Know ye the truth and the truth shall set you free.

What allows us to enter the Gateway of Knowing? When Jesus said, "Know ye the truth and the truth shall set you free;" what truth did he mean and what did he mean by know? The Bible was not yet written, and the vast majority of his followers were illiterate. What did He mean by truth?

What if Jesus meant we must find the truth that lies within us? The "Christic fractal" as Barbara Marx Hubbard calls it, is the part of us that has soul intelligence and a clear sense of what is congruent with our knowing. What is sometimes mistaken for conscience is in actuality a deep spiritual inner connection and alignment with harmony and justice, that I deem Knowing.

It is this knowing that motivated Mother Teresa to go to India. It motivated a weary Rosa Parks to say no to giving up her seat on the bus. It inspired Gandhi to march to the sea in protest of the salt tax. Great souls like Nelson Mandela and Aung San Suu Kyi suffered years of trauma, persecution, and tribulation because of their steadfast commitment to knowing a truth they needed to honor and protect.

I asked Mother Mary to offer a message about how we can truly Know:

Be Still and Know.
This is the essence of peace.
Be Still and Know.
There is a Way and you can find it.
Be Still and Know.
I am with you.

In the midst of your pain, there is an answer. In the midst of confusion, there is a quiet place. In the midst of all, there is the Presence that made you and knows you and would bring you Home. All that is required is your willingness and a choice to be still. In this sacred pause, your knowing, and your light can illuminate the cause of your confusion and you will Know that you are free to choose a more loving Path.

What has this life brought to you? What have you brought to this life? What haunts you, touches you, and calls your name in the night? It is

I. It is you. It is the force that binds us and bounds us and will not let you go. It is our love and our boundless joy in who you are and what you bring that infuses your every breath with the holiness of our love. I have come again to remind you of what you may have forgotten.

You are a holy being in a human life. You are a radiant angel with heavenly wings walking amidst the splendors of an earth that is so beautiful and precious, of all of the planets, we chose this place to feed our light.

Why have I come in this way at this time? To call you home: To call you to the glories and the radiance of your true name. Your name is Light. Your name is Love. Your name is "my child" and "my dear one" and "my love."

I have come to remind you of all of the promises that you have felt in your life and all of the loneliness that you have endured as you searched for the food that would nourish your soul.

I have come with glad tidings and immense joy to say, amen, and welcome to the new kingdom, the kingdom of heaven on earth that is being birthed as we infuse this world with the light that transforms all into radiance and readiness.

It is time, dear one. It is time. As you have walked upon this earth and felt the wonder and the pain, you grew. You have found treasures in your life along with the disappointments and disillusionment. Now it is time for the greatest treasure you will ever know. This is the treasure of your true nature: the vast wealth of your expression; the abundance of your light and the alchemy of the most precious substance of all: your love.

There is a price to be paid for this holy inheritance. It is time to give up your addictions. It is time to disavow the lies and compromise of convenience. It is time to stand up for what you believe and to share what you know. And how shall you Know?

You must take the time to find stillness in your day and to sit with the presence that feeds you, nourishes you, and knows your truth. Sit with a candle. Sit with lovely music. Sit in the cathedral or the forest or the church down the road. Sit with your mind still and your heart open. Be still and know.

And what will you know? You will know your true nature. You will know where you have stopped your life force from dancing. You will know how you are suffocating your spirit. You will know how you have hidden from your friends and your family and your loved ones, the deepest treasures of your heart.

Be still and know. This is the first of the steps that will bring you Home again. I call to you and entreat you to find the time and the space. You may not feel it is a worthy endeavor. You may feel silly, irresponsible, self-conscious, bored, tired, or lazy. All of that is the conditioning of a mind that has been taught to disavow its grander nature.

Comfort this fearful part and allow the peace to fill you with a new thought.

"I came to make a difference."

"I came to share my love and my light with joy and grace and wisdom." "I came to sing."

"I came to soar." "I came to shine."
That is your true heart's calling. Let that voice sing in your life.

The first step, dear ones, is: Be Still and Know.

It is the practice and the premise that within you lies the wealth of many kingdoms. It is your right and your choice to open the treasure. Once you have found this fountain of love and certainty within you, you may delight in the sharing of it with all that would be exalted by your love and inspired by your knowing.

Be Still and Know… I am with you.

I wondered if there was a time when Mother Mary came to the Gateway of Knowing and what she experienced when she had to live in a new land. I asked her to share her experience.

Although our small group was not often in the company of others, there were new moments for me. Jesus came often and taught me what was to come when I joined him in the next realm. His early messages of love and brotherhood and possibility had indeed planted the seeds of change. Yet, as he shared with me, much would still have to occur in the years still to come.

He told me that there would be numerous ways that I would touch the humanity that was still awakening. I smiled at this thought in amusement and disbelief. And yet, as I had throughout my life, I agreed to follow the Path that would be revealed as a deep knowing touched my heart and brought peace to the questions still unresolved in my mind.

Another way to further develop our Knowing is to ask, "With the gifts and talents that I have, what can I do to help the struggling, amazing birth that is happening?"

Then, we must take the steps our guidance suggests. This soul path requires we bring our full soul presence, what Harvey called our "embodied divinity," into our present experience. There is extraordinarily little assurance of what tomorrow might bring. The usual human planning for the future with the five- and ten-year goals of a linear mind no longer applies. There can be a lovely return to the innocence of the child, who wakes up and leaps out of bed, ready for a new day and a new set of experiences.

This is what Jesus meant when he said, "You must become as little children to enter the kingdom of heaven." Letting go of the approval of others, and simply being present, brought joy and reminders that heaven is with us when we open to light. Mary indicated there was a mission for me at the Chalice Well in Glastonbury, England. Unsure of what was to be asked of me, I simply knew I was to go.

As part of a delegation of the Madonna Ministry, we booked our trip to Glastonbury, a very mystical and sacred place, home of the Chalice Well and the Tor, and a great deal of history. I traveled with my trusty friend Diane. We excitedly boarded our plane in Phoenix and set off for England. Once we arrived at Heathrow Airport, we made our way to Glastonbury, which involved two trains and a very slow-moving bus.

By the time we arrived in Glastonbury in the drizzling rain, jet lag had set in, and we were both struggling with a lack of sleep and a sense of disorientation. We grabbed our bags and disembarked from the bus. Examining our map, we saw that the bed-and-breakfast where we had arranged to stay was a few blocks walk. On we went, covering our heads as best we could from the relentless English rain. We made it up the hill and knocked on the door. No answer. We knocked more loudly. No answer. We stood there in the rain, disheveled, disappointed, and exhausted. I looked up at the sky and said a simple prayer, "Please help us, Mother Mary. I don't know what we are going to do now."

My friend and I looked at each other and looked back down the street where we had gotten off the bus and decided to walk back to wait inside the café, as perhaps the owner of the B and B had simply stepped out for a few minutes.

As we walked, I saw a woman walking toward us and for a moment I thought, oh that must be her. Thank you, Mother Mary! As the woman came closer, she was not moving toward the doorway of the B and B. I sighed and looked heavenward. And then I heard, "Samarah? Is that you?" There, in the streets of Glastonbury, thousands of miles from home, stood a woman I had met in Sedona several years prior at the Madonna Ministry conference. I could not help but laugh. What were the chances of someone walking up the exact street in Glastonbury where my friend and I were standing, just when we needed help and that this someone would know me and remember my name? Thank you, Mother Mary!

Dear Elizabeth grabbed the handle of my suitcase and walked us back to the tearoom. She knew our host and said she had gone out of town for a couple of days and there was no one else who could let us in. We did not have a reservation or a cell phone. Elizabeth took over and found us a place to stay for the night. She then helped us get our luggage to the hotel and left us to sink into a deep slumber and peaceful dreams, knowing the power of prayer and the gentle touch of Mother Mary can indeed bring all kinds of miracles.

The next day, our embarrassed host returned and made us comfortable, letting us know she had written the wrong date for our arrival. We were just relieved to be in her extremely sweet and lovely apartment and readied ourselves for the day. The main event for the first day was to go to the Chalice Well Gardens and do a ceremony.

Mother Mary asked me to do a special ceremony at the Chalice Well and specifically over the vesica piscis cover. Mother Mary told me years ago, when the patriarchy overran the gentle grace of the feminine, the priestesses had sealed the sacred codes of the feminine power energies beneath the well to preserve them. It was time now for them to be released and thus begin a reawakening of the divine feminine power and lineage. I had learned by now not to question too deeply what I was to do or what would be involved. I had learned certain energy patterns of love and blessing, and Reiki could dispel the darker energies of fear and domination. As a willing participant, with focus and intention, I could be a vehicle for that offering. All over the world for centuries, the feminine energies have been treated with disregard and suppression. Emissaries of Light are being asked to lift these repressive patterns as we receive help and instructions from the angelic realms.

It was a cloudy day, and the Chalice Well Gardens had the usual crowd of people walking around. I wondered how I could do what I had been asked to do amid the others. I sat on a bench, closed my eyes, said a prayer I was willing to do what was asked of me and to show me how and when. It began to drizzle and then rain steadily, and the crowd scattered for cover. I smiled at the mystery of how things work and walked over to the chalice well cover. I raised my arms and then moved them as shown, releasing the codes that had sealed the well to protect the sacred essence within. It took but a few minutes and I could feel the energy swirling and moving. I offered another prayer of gratitude and made my way out of the garden.

Later that day, we were doing a ceremony in St. Michaels Chapel. I would channel Mother Mary's message and there would be a consecration of new ministers who were joining the Madonna Ministry. We entered the tiny chapel, and I made my way to the front, where I would speak. As we were settling in, four women peeked in the doorway and asked, "What are you doing here and are we allowed to enter?" They were from Holland on holiday in Glastonbury and had felt the energy of Mary and been drawn to where we were. I motioned for them to enter and told them they could stay as long as they liked and leave whenever they felt it was time.

Mother Mary's Message echoed the unseen energy which had guided the Dutch women into our meeting and truly to all of us who follow a Path that is often the road less traveled.

Greetings to all my beloveds. Today I would like to clear up any misunderstandings you may still have about who is in charge of change for you and your planet. I hear all your requests and prayers and I send streams of light and inspiration. And yet it is for you to act in the direction of love, peace, harmony, and compassion. It is time to move out of despair, apathy, fear, and reluctance. It is time for you to choose and act with honor and courage.

Mary continued to encourage each of us to function as we are guided and ended by offering a beautiful transmission of healing energy.

The Dutch delegation stayed for the entire message and ceremony and afterward introduced themselves and thanked us. One woman was the publisher of a spiritual magazine called *Powwow*. She invited me to share Mother Mary's channeling for the next issue of her magazine, and I agreed.

Later I would laughingly tell my friends now "Mother Mary was in Dutch" (a colloquialism for being in trouble!)

Back home in Arizona, the miracles continued. Serena and I had the joy and blessing of yet another visitation from Mother Mary. Serena had asked me to do a private 1-1 Reiki training for her. We returned to the beauty of Sedona and booked a room at Poco Diablo resort. It was a beautiful fall Saturday. We had spent the day in the beauty of Fay Canyon and Bell Rock where I had offered her the Reiki teachings and attunements. We returned to the room and rested, and suddenly we both arose, as if a bell had sounded. We looked at each other and knew we had to go outside.

Poco Diablo has lovely weeping willow trees on the grounds, and we were drawn to one gigantic tree that emanated a very particular invitation. We stood under the tree nestled in her embrace. Suddenly, we both stepped back and looked again at the tree as something had palpably shifted. We both felt Mother Mary, who seemed to over-light the tree with a powerful and loving energy. It was as if Mary was the tree, and the tree was Mary. The branches were her arms, and the emanation was fragrant and powerful.

We looked at each other for confirmation, and both of us knew we were again being blessed by Mary. We stood there for another few minutes. Tears of gratitude and grace fell silently and there were no words. Then, Mary spoke to me, and I shared the message with Serena.

Many ask to see me and beseech me for the healing that would bring them peace. What you have both realized is that I am speaking to any who have called and urging them to go where their heart has called them.

For both of you who initially resisted the call of Reiki, now you see that Reiki is one path to Home. To say yes to Reiki is to say I am willing to be changed. I am willing to see. I am willing to know, and I am willing to offer myself as a light when I am called by those who still dwell in the darkness of their own making.

I am here to say thank you to both of you for not only hearing the call, but having the courage to follow where it would lead. Much lies ahead for both of you.

Let this experience live in your heart and your memory so when there is doubt or fear of what to do, you will know that when you choose what the soul and heart are requesting, miracles await.

I wish finding the Knowing gateway and allowing all that unfolds could somehow lead to a Zen-like enduring peace, but that has not been my experience. The analogy I would use is when we learn to trust our Knowing, we become like an expert surfer or martial artist. With experience and trust, we become more centered and prepared for whatever may come. We may still be defeated by an unexpected wave or assailant, but we can quickly regain our composure. At this gateway, we must sacrifice the momentary Approval that following the more traditional path brings, but the gift is a deep and lasting Peace.

THE SEVENTH GATEWAY:
Surrendering to the Light
Crown Chakra
The Sacrifice: Control
The Gift: Innocence

I Am Blessed

At this Gateway, you enter the realm of soul embodiment, no longer held captive by your biology or conditioning. Your soul star radiates and communicates with you. Your heart knows which direction is for you. Your central "gut" chakra reacts to each choice, and you feel the path of light that offers profound joy. You have become again like a little child, innocent and unafraid, ready to be a blessing and to be blessed.

Surrender is often misunderstood and seen as a sign of weakness. We imagine a white flag being raised and having to submit to a conqueror. What I have found is the humble act of soul surrender can bring freedom and a peace that, occasionally, will open the door for miracles. I surrendered, not to Mother Mary as a ruling authority, but to the light my soul had found. I gave up looking for the world's approval or asking others to show me their "guaranteed" Path to success. There is a deep peace in knowing I am simply living my inner light's direction, always asking just one question, "What would love do here?" At this gateway, we must sacrifice Control to gain the gift of *Innocence.*

Caroline Myss offers a thoughtful explanation of Surrender in her groundbreaking book, *Anatomy of the Spirit.* Myss suggests, "Putting faith in human justice is an error and we must shift our faith from human to Divine Authority." As part of reaching out and connecting with like-minded spiritual seekers, I had learned about an energy healing modality known as Reiki. One of my friends was a Usui Reiki Master and head of the International Reiki Institute offering classes in Arizona and around the world. I had always respected her but had no interest in pursuing Reiki. As with so much in my life, once you hear the call from Spirit, it is best to listen and surrender to the Divine Mind that guides us all.

When my guidance had first come to take Reiki, I held back, feeling stubborn and stuck in my logical mind, I was never going to be a "direct" healer. Still, my guidance kept whispering and urging me to take Reiki 1. So, despite my reluctance, as the famous Borg episode on Star Trek offered, "Resistance is futile."

I can truthfully share arguing with Spirit is not only futile, but it also blocks the miracles that await the Path those in the higher realms are lighting up. All kidding aside, once the idea is offered, if it is for your highest good, the unseen angels and guides will start flooding your life with hints, subtle and not so subtle. Friends will keep bringing you stories about Reiki. You will see flyers for Reiki classes. You will see the word "Reiki" in emails and on TV. It becomes as persistent as a toddler after a cookie. It has become my experience surrendering early is a far better use of our time and energy.

After weeks of nonstop Reiki suggestions in 1997, I enrolled in the next Reiki 1 class, believing that would be the end. As we gathered for the class, I felt a thickness in the air. Sophia called in the Lineage of Light of the Usui Reiki lineage, which included Dr Usui, Mr. Hayashi, and Mrs. Takata, along with the 22 Masters trained by Mrs. Takata. I felt the electricity in the air and knew something huge was about to change my life again. Reiki I includes learning technique and being attuned by the Master. The Reiki Master Teachers put their hands on each student and channel energy and symbols to awaken the Reiki energy.

As I sat there waiting my turn, I sensed a vast circle of beings who have served to light this world for eons. I was being brought into a lineage of light whose purpose was to teach and touch all who came with the infinite light of love. I felt humbled, happy, and excited. As my Reiki Master put her hands on my head, I felt my crown chakra blast open and a pouring in of knowing and love and expansion. Tears streamed down my face and time stopped. Then, as my Reiki Master stood in front of me and took my hands, I felt them grow hot and dissolve as if my body were melting. I had come home to a lineage of world servers and now I could serve as well.

Later I would realize you do not choose Reiki; it chooses you when you feel ready to know everyone you meet creates an opportunity to offer love and healing. It is a way of being as well as a healing modality. Over the years, it has become much more widely known and accepted. It is used now in many hospitals to ease pain and speed healing. Many hospices provide Reiki to comfort patients and help them transition.

Despite my initial reluctance, the power and love I had experienced led me to continue my Reiki training. I took Reiki 2 and 3, then completed a year as an apprentice to become a Reiki Teaching Master. In this process, I was continually challenged to let go of my old logical way of trying to control and evaluate things, and trust in the inner guidance that would often ask me to do things when my logical brain could not see any validity in that choice.

A case in point would be the cost of becoming a Usui Reiki Master with a traditional teacher. Mrs. Takata had set the amount of $10,000 back in the 1970s. Those who were following this guideline continued to charge this amount, and that is what my Reiki Master charged. There were many discount Masters and programs available. However, my guidance was this Path of the original integrity and lineage was the one for me. I let my logical mind kick and scream for a while with thoughts like "There is no such thing as a human Master outside oneself." "I could do this on my own." " I don't want to be under anyone as an apprentice." And on and on it went for a while.

Finally, I surrendered to the inner knowing and the feeling this was to be my Path. I arranged a payment plan I could manage, and we began. As part of my apprenticeship, I assisted at each Reiki class and practiced giving the Reiki attunements. When my Reiki Master was invited to Switzerland and Germany to teach, I went with her to learn how to offer Reiki with a translator, and how to do attunements with those who do not speak the same language.

It was an intense year of training in the art of surrendering and being open to all that was possible in reaching the other realms. My experiences channeling Mother Mary and my training as a Reiki Master teacher wove together, as I could hold higher and higher frequencies for longer and longer periods. In the beginning of channeling Mother Mary, I could only hold her frequency for a few minutes, and then felt exhausted from the effort. As my Reiki training and experience continued, I could now hold the energy for hours at a time and felt exhilarated rather than exhausted by the communion.

I became a Usui Reiki Teaching Master four months after the first visitation from Mother Mary. My Master attunement took place in Sedona, Arizona, in the sacred canyon next to the Enchantment Resort, where the Native Guardian Spirits witnessed my promise to love and serve for the highest good for all. I feel my choice to follow spirit rather than logic, and to commit myself to the Path of Reiki, however challenging financially and energetically, opened Pathways in me which allowed Mother Mary to come into my life and offer me a Path to love and grace.

My commitment to Surrender and living in unconditional love, along with the support of a tight-knit spiritual group I was leading, led to another miracle we had the privilege of witnessing. I held an annual *Dare to Dream* retreat at the Merritt Center in Payson, Arizona. It was a very fitting choice since the center had been created after the founder, Betty Merritt, had dared to dream.

Betty was working as vice president for a company where she managed eleven offices from San Francisco to New York and found herself on an airplane four days a week. After having a spiritual experience on a Shiatsu table, she heard a voice say, "Let go." Her call to Awakening, Discovery, and Commitment all converged at that moment.

She quit her job the next week and started on a journey to create a space for people to let go and learn from their stressful experiences. Seeking guidance where she might locate this space, she saw a field overflowing with purple and yellow pansies. Startled and confused by this vision, she asked for more specifics, but the pansies continued. She finally surrendered to this persistent and puzzling vision and left to find this elusive field of pansies.

In June 1987, after driving 36,000 miles, she discovered a quiet country retreat with a backyard full of purple and yellow Johnny Jump Ups that looked like baby pansies. There she founded The Merritt Center, as the culmination of her dream to provide a space for people to experience renewal and empowerment.

I knew Betty's dream space would be the perfect place to help participants find new ways to be in the world that felt more authentic and offered more joy. When Mother Mary first spoke of why she had come, she indicated we could learn again how to create miracles, or "remedies," as she referred to them. At this Dare to Dream gathering, we would be challenged to create a remedy for a difficult and very troubling situation.

One woman had received news that during her daughter's latest ultrasound, the doctors found lesions on the brain of her unborn granddaughter. They had gravely advised brain damage was probable, and the doctors were genuinely concerned about the extent of issues she might have.

As Val tearfully shared this heartbreaking news, I knew we needed to gather all of our strength and concentrate the light to send to this little soul. Val lay down on the floor and we handed her a large teddy bear to stand in as the baby. She clutched it to her. We said a prayer for the highest good and asked the soul of this child to hear and receive our prayers and healing energy. I offered to speak to the soul of the child and asked to be guided what words might have influence. This was our act of Surrender to divine will and divine love.

Then it was as if I climbed a staircase into another realm. I could feel the little one's fear about coming into this world. She knew how difficult and challenging the energies of the earth had become and was unsure she could manage. I said, "You are so loved. You are so wanted. We need you to come and to be healthy and happy. We will stand with you (all of us) as your godmothers. We will advise and help you whenever you need us. Come, dear little one, and know you are safe."

The air in the room took on a holy sweetness. Everyone was sending love and prayers of strength and peace. Val stopped crying and was holding the teddy bear with a look of deep peace on her face. When the transmission felt complete, I put my arms down and took the hands of those next to me.

We formed a circle around Val and sang "Amazing Grace." There were tears, and yet there was also a sense something extraordinary had occurred from joining together and offering this concentration of light. Val slowly got up and thanked us and you could see hope had supplanted the fear which had filled her before we began. Three months later, little Alexa was born without any sign of lesions. She is perfect. That was nine years ago, and she now has a baby sister, loves volleyball, and is a sweet and precious light. It was a miracle we will always celebrate and give thanks for.

I share these miracles of change to show the enormous and transformative power of love I have witnessed. Surrender is not passive. It requires being fully present and ready to respond with love. When Mother Mary first appeared in my living room all those years ago, her question to me was, "Will you be with me?" I did not know how powerful truly being with someone could be. For Val and her unborn granddaughter, and for all those who have been touched by Mother Mary, we are forever changed.

Mary's unconditional love we are learning to receive, and give is not dependent upon outer approval or recognition. It is hearing the call of the heart and then offering that into the world. As Mother Mary reminded me, the mantra to live by is:

As I honor me; so, I honor thee.

We must first respect, love, and honor ourselves, filling our hearts and minds and bodies with the nurturance we require. Then, when we give to others, it is from our authenticity and our fullness. In the words of Jesus, "Love thy neighbor as thyself" reminds us loving ourselves is a necessary part of the equation. Thus, as we surrender to our own truth and knowing, we can regain our innocence and become again as little children to enter the kingdom.

Seeing a vision of Mary is a rare and precious event. I feel blessed that three of the four times I have seen her, others were with me who witnessed Mary and also felt the touch of her grace. I do think it is important to question things we do not understand. I also believe the ridicule and censure the Marian visionaries experienced is one more reminder of how much courage, stamina, and faith they had to walk the Path that seeing Mother requires.

In the twenty-two years of devotion to Mother Mary and her messages, I have spoken with religious and lay people and each one who has a devotion to Mary feels it is their Mary who speaks to them. That is one sign of what a remarkable mother she is. We each believe we are her most precious child. Held in her all-encompassing embrace, Mary invites us to rise to our highest potential and create a world we are proud to live in and offer as our legacy to future generations.

I know we are not alone, and I feel blessed to have watched the power of love create miracles of healing and community. I believe Mother Mary will stay with us, urging us onward, reminding us we are each here to ignite the soul light within and find a joyous way to share that light with others. It is finally time to awaken and fulfill the dream Mother Mary holds for all of us.

Heaven is not a place of refuge for those of us who wish to continue our service. I do not sit on a cloud with a harp and wings. I dream a dream that one day each of you will know how much you are loved and stand with great courage and authority and say Yes to a life of love. You see me in gardens and buildings, and you hear me in the meadows, fields, and forests. You pray to me and beseech me to intercede in your lives and lift any suffering. I hear every prayer and I give thanks for every rosary and yet this is not my dream.

My dream is that you will awaken and seize this life as your creation and your story to write. My dream is that you will gather with others and create patterns of kindness and community. My dream is that you will not rest in a world filled with inequity and suffering. My dream is that you will know your power as well as your compassion.

Jesus told his disciples and followers over two thousand years ago that all that he did, they could do and more. My dream is that you will believe him and begin.

You are my hands and my heart in the world. Become the dream I have held and create the new garden that offers rest and comfort and peace to all.

Each journey through the seven gateways is not linear with a final completion. It is an ever-evolving spiral with more Awakening, more Discovery, more Commitment, more Tribulation, more Rebirth, more Knowing and more Surrender. The periods of forgetting who we are, become briefer and the upsets life brings do not occur as frequently or last as long. Prayer, meditation, time in nature, all the spiritual practices we choose can assist us in offering our joyous presence in the world. Compassion, kindness, service, and peace are the new currency for this way of being.

It is worth the challenges of each gateway. We sacrifice *Safety, Security, Certainty, Comfort, Belonging, Approval and Control. The gifts we receive of Courage, Trust, Passion, Compassion, Authenticity, Peace, and Innocence are precious and priceless.* We become again as little children in the garden of life, sheltered by our knowing, sovereign souls, certain of our light.

Section 3
Remedies for a Troubled World

From Mother Mary

My dearest Emissaries of Light
This is a time in your history when you must decide what your future will hold. For centuries you have relied upon the wisdom and training of others to mold the world you inhabit. Now as you clear away the illusions you can find the voice of your heart and your knowing. This truth as it grows stronger will guide you in co creating a world that cannot allow children to starve while silos full of grain are left to rot. You will no longer allow old men and women to die alone without comfort. You will no longer allow air and water to be polluted in the name of progress. Be the chalice of love. Be the bringer of hope. Take the actions that call to you. It is time and we are with you.
Every act of violence perpetrated upon the innocent stems from the wrongly held belief that it is your brother (the other) who keeps you from that which you seek. You want what they have, and you do not believe in your own capacity to create it. Thus, you will steal or kill or harm in your misplaced and frantic desire to get what you believe will give you peace or power.

To live as a sovereign soul, no longer at the mercy of the paradigm of victim, perpetrator, and rescuer, I offer these suggestions to invite a new understanding.

The Sandy Hook shooting 12/12

My dearest ones. In this time of shock and sadness, please understand the nature of light and darkness. The young man who killed first his mother, and then the children and the others at the school did not know how to deal with his despair and darkness. He felt isolated and wronged and wanted to do something to feel alive and to prove he had power. He was seeking his own lost innocence. He went to the youngest ones in a fury of rage and hatred as they held what he so desperately wanted to find.

The tiny innocent souls that died at the school sacrificed their future and their innocence in the hope that many would begin to see, feel the vast loneliness, and despair that so many others face. Violence will end when there is liberty and justice for all and when each being grows up, knowing they have value and a way to share who they are with this world that is meaningful.

What all of you can do is hold a vision of a world in which every child is safe and held in the embrace of family and community. Hold a vision where what is valued is discovering the gifts and graces each being has and where each being is encouraged to find the path of joy that allows them to share their contribution. Envision a world that assists all beings to have a life that provides them with connection and meaning.

My dearest ones, this is a time for prayer and for dedicating a new vision.Imagine a world where there is a place at the table for everyone who comes in peace. Reach out to those who are angry and disenfranchised and help them to find a way to heal the hatred that poisons their hearts and leads to such desperate acts.

A new paradigm can be birthed. A new world of inclusion and love can be created. There can be no safety or freedom while there is tyranny anywhere in the world. The new vision can be born as you imagine what is needed and choose the actions that flow from that vision. It can be done, and we are with you.

The Global Pandemic Illness and Pain

Pain and suffering are not inflicted by God or any of us. We do not wish pain for anyone. Yet we do wish to offer a way of seeing it that may be of assistance. There is within each of you a consciousness that is your spiritual guidance system. Like the black box on an airplane, it records and yet it is much more. It measures the disparity between what you require for joy and growth, and what you are choosing.

Your world seldom encourages the examination of that black box until there is a malfunction or catastrophe. In a world where the exhaustion that occurs from the endless quest for more is seen as laudatory, the inner voice of alignment is seen as an obstacle to success. Thus, it is the body that will find a way to reach you. Pain gets your attention. Pain causes you to stop for a while. Pain causes you to examine the choices you are making to see if they are for your highest good. If you simply drown out the pain with medications or addictions, it will return. The purpose of the pain is to get your attention and invite an assessment of your choices. Perhaps ask the question, what would bring more ease into my body and my life? See what arises.

If it is a child that is suffering, the remedy is in the hands of the family and medical community that is called to attend. The child is not responsible for choosing or creating the conditions. It is for the parents and others to see how they can heal the disparity or simply find the path of greatest light, compassion, and healing.

The global pandemic is a clarion call to the population of earth. What are you choosing that allows such social and economic disparity? If you do not care for those who have so little, their breath of despair and hopelessness becomes the air you breathe. If they live without clean water, soon your water will also be filled with contaminants.

For centuries, the powerful have built castle walls protected by guards and moats. Others have security fences, guards, and gates. None of that will work in a contaminated and uncared for world.

Add to that a lack of trust in your governments, in vaccines, and in each other. Some of that is well founded from past misconduct, and yet much of it is simply fear, misinformation, and a desire to circle the wagons to protect your own domain.

The answer is not simple. First, you must trust yourself and honor your connection to your Spirit and higher self. Armed with this knowing, you will discern what is best for you. Next, decide that you will do your best to heal the global disparity. If you decide not to have the vaccine, contribute what you can to those desperate for that protection. Be respectful to those who have made a different choice. Blaming and shaming simply contribute to the toxicity that created the dilemma. It is one world and all of you are breathing the same air and drinking the same water.

The remedy for pain, illness, and pandemics is the same. Face what is being experienced. Center yourself and connect with the highest light you know. Dispense with opinions that are mired in fear. Choose the path of greatest love. Fill your life with clarity, beauty, and peace. Then offer compassion, kindness, understanding and what resources you can to the global community. It can be prayer, blankets, money, time. Be part of the balm of healing. Be the kindness.

In a world where there is enough food, peace, and opportunity for everyone, there is no longer a need to wield the ancient hammers of power or react from fear that you will not have enough.

Death

Death is not a punishment. It is our promise to you that you will come home to us. Each soul lives in the world until their assignment is complete. Sometimes that is for decades; sometimes it is for the briefest of times. If you fear death, you have not begun to understand the nature of incarnation.

You come to earth with unique seeds of promise and possibility. Which seeds you plant and nurture determine the garden of your life. Connecting to the elements of earth and water, air and fire allows for balance of new growth, harvesting of that which is ripe, and plowing under what is complete.

As any farmer will tell you, there are forces of nature and cataclysmic events that can decimate what you have worked so hard to create. In those moments, you are challenged to reach inward and call upon the qualities within you that you have nurtured. Are you resilient? Creative? Powerful? Loving? Do you have friendships and support to rebuild and go on?

You will decide. Knowing this, look to those you love and how you may celebrate and share the bounty and beauty of all you grow. Each soul is doing their best. If you have bounty to share; share it that they too might have a garden that feeds and nourishes them and their loved ones.

Death is a promise. What you choose to grow is what will be in the garden of your lifetime.

What happens after death?

For all who have worried and wondered, I offer this promise. No one is denied entrance into the ocean of all souls. There is a time of reflection for those who never learned the laws of love. It as if you are taken into a lovely comfortable waiting room. You are offered rest and refreshment. When you are ready, you watch a movie of your life. You see all of the opportunities to give and receive love. You see where you did, and where you did not. There is no judgment, simply an awakening within.

When your time for reflection is complete, you are offered an opportunity to stay or to return to earth. It is always your choice. Many do return, determined to rectify any lost opportunities. Some ask to be in touch with family or friends that they would like to make amends with.

Live your lives fully. Love deeply. Share with kindness and generosity. Forgive with compassion. Then, when you are here with us watching your movie, you will smile and be drenched in contentment.

Soul Fulfillment

Greed, Disparity, and Neglect are the true enemies of fulfillment. There are three more streams of thought that slow the progress and harvest you seek: Resistance, Reluctance and Regret.

Your soul star holds the seeds of your promise, your purpose, and your possibilities. Once you access this stream, you will be guided to the areas and resources that can provide fulfillment.

The dreams of the earth lie within each of you. As you heal the conditioning that inhibits your knowing, more energy is released and magnetized to your deepest wishes. You will encounter resistance, reluctance, and regret as you break free of longing for or needing the approval of others. The priceless rewards are freedom, peace, and authenticity,

These are not the dreams of material wealth and power that so many have sought. These are the soul dreams of a bountiful earth and a thriving humanity and an end to the desperation, deception, and degradation wrought by greed, disparity, and neglect. You are now curious, clear, connected, creative, conscious, courageous, confident, calm and most of all congruent with your choice to be an Emissary of Light. The New Garden awaits.

Soul Purpose and Creativity.

Your creativity is far more glorious than you know. It is the opportunity in every moment to bring your ideas, your heart, your feelings, your very body into whatever involvement you would like or choose. What has happened on the earth, especially in the last one hundred years, is that beings get a little lost trying to make money. They feel they must do this by following a script that was given to them by their teachers or their parents or their counselors or their husbands or wives. They believed if they followed a script, they would know the beginning and the middle and the end. They would work for this employer for 40 years and at the end, they would receive this beautiful gold watch and go off to Florida and live happily ever after. I am not saying that this was a dreadful thing or a wrong thing.

What I am saying is you could have a far more interesting story to tell. When you follow a script that is given to you from someone else, 90% of you shuts down. Think about that. What happens is the 10% that is left does a more than adequate job of following the script and doing what you are told. But the rest of you that is dormant begins to rise up with impatience, concern, unhappiness, and sometimes illness. What it tells you in your dreams or in your walks on the beach or in a special moment is you are greater than this. There is more for you. There is more. We are waiting. And yet you are being a good person. You are following the script you were given. Your joy begins to be squeezed into a smaller and smaller fraction of your life. Your spontaneity and creativity are squeezed. You feel heavier, shuttered, depressed.

What I have come to remind you will not come as a shocking surprise. If you decide to write your own script, parts of you will come to life with joy, rapture, and excitement. But meanwhile the other that has been following the script will often be frightened and say oh you must not do that! You must not do that! You must not do that!

And so, because it is all God, it is not about throwing away that part of you. It is about changing the equation. You begin to think, what did I come here to do. Did I come to spend 40 years at the same job to have a gold watch and go to Florida? Is that really what I came to do? And if it is enjoy!

But if it is not, what you are abandoning is your purpose, your fire, your love, and your gifts. You are abandoning a lot of your goodness if you do not develop what is calling to you. Each being before they came to this life sat and thought what they could bring to the planet of earth. You wrote a script before you came, and it is that script that is wanting to be noticed by you.

Ask what was I born to do? If you return to your childhood, you will think back to certain moments, certain events, certain circumstances, and you will remember who you are in an incredibly distinct way. You will begin to see that there is a script that you wrote before you came that wants to dance, that wants to sing, that wants to play. Listen to your heart. The world can be a very heavy taskmaster. Take stock of yourself, and ask what would I love to do? If it is dancing and you have not danced in 10 years, could you spend 5 minutes a day dancing? If you missed the solitude of the mountains believing it is too far to go, or takes too much time, find the place that brings you into joy. There will always be someone demanding from you that you follow their script. And I tell you this, if you cannot fulfill your own purpose, your heart closes and soon you have nothing left to give. You are meant to have a life you love that also serves the world. Find your joy. Become a vessel for it. Fill yourself to overflowing and offer that elixir to a thirsty world.

Innocence

To become as a little child again is not to deny whatever betrayal or hardships you have endured. It is to seek, find, and allow a breath of joy to fill your heart. Walk in the forest or by the sea. Make beautiful art or play music. Cuddle with your child or your pet. Go somewhere new and let its beauty restore your imagination. Find the place in you that is ever pure and precious.

All beings require renewal. The past holds regret; the future holds uncertainty. It is in the present that you can find true joy. Delight in its myriad colors and shapes, fragrances, and feelings. You will miss them when you come home to us.

There is great power in your innocence. When you live from that pure place, you will not judge and react to your own stumbling or that of others. The accusations and reprisals of the past will be a distant memory. Instead, you will see that everyone is doing what they believe will serve them. Compassion will replace the harshness of condemnation. Your gentleness becomes a healing balm of forgiveness and new possibilities.

Discernment

Discernment is not judgment. It is wisdom and experience. To see yourself and other clearly allows for choices to be made that move you always in the direction of love and authenticity. If someone has little regard for your wellbeing, your choice is to move aside and set them free from your life. If someone lies to you or cheats, it is important to not look away.

Reacting in anger or simmering rage is also not advisable. Allow yourself time to become clear and calm. Tell them what they have done and how you feel about it. Listen to their response. If it is one of denial or excuses, decide if you will offer one more chance or if it is time to simply say, that does not work for me. To live as a sovereign soul, honesty and clarity are essential. Abuse erodes your heart and compromises your confidence.

I invite you to consider a new mantra, "As I honor me; so, I honor thee."

Forgiveness

All that I have offered will be of no value if you do not learn forgiveness. To set free those who have wronged you is not for their benefit. It is for yours. Each injury that you allow to remain is a place held in the past, held in judgment and sorrow, held in anger and disappointment. Imagine that each one prevents the glorious flow of vitality and joy. Each is a weight that you carry that impedes your freedom and your expression.

At the end of Jesus' life, on the cross, suffering a most unspeakable death, he cried out, "Father, forgive them for they know not what they do." In that moment, his body no longer held the wounds of betrayal and misunderstanding. He was free.

I promise you that despite the ills you have suffered, your place is with us. You have never been forsaken, forgotten, punished, or ignored. Indeed, you have been touched and guided and held to our hearts all the times you thought yourself alone, as well as the times you knew your glory.

Whatever still holds you in regret, let it go. Forgive yourself for any and all the times you did not choose love. Let them all go. Take a breath and now choose again. Let this be your new way of being: I am an Emissary of Light, on an earthly mission of Love. I am a sovereign soul sharing my gifts with courage, trust, passion, compassion, authenticity, peace, and innocence. So, it is.

Samarah's Remedies:
My Journey from Guarded to Guided.

My dearest family of light,

Once we have freed our light from the conditioning of earthly habit and judgment, we can live as Emissaries of Light. It is in our hands to bring the power of our light to create remedies for this troubled world. The journey through the seven gateways helped me to shift from seeing life only from my human biography to seeing through the eyes of my soul.

What helped me immensely was to see that my story could be transformed as I took greater and greater responsibility. I could choose my response from the old paradigm of a powerless victim or shift my focus of choice to the possibilities available to a sovereign soul. I was the author, and I could ask myself the question, What is the story I am telling myself? What is the story those I am interacting with are telling themselves? Is it a conscious choice? An outworn belief?

For much of humanity's history, power was used to dominate, not liberate. We have been locked in a paradigm defined by the subjugation of the weaker by the more powerful. Worth is measured in acquisitions of money, land, and military might. In this way of life, there are victims, perpetrators, rescuers, and silent onlookers.

The degradation of the planet and the ongoing suffering of much of the world's population has been the outcome. Whatever our political beliefs or social standing, consider it may be time for a new paradigm of co-creation and harmony of being. I believe we must become sovereign by examining what we believe and what we know. Where are we still dividing? Blaming? Excluding?

If you felt the call and agreed to live as an Emissary of Light, we are being asked to move out of judgment and reaction and choose equanimity, kindness, compassion, and generosity.

Ram Dass exemplified this path for me. At one of his retreats, he was addressing concerns and questions. One man was clearly torn about how much time he could devote to his spiritual studies when he had a full-time job, a wife, and two children to support. He wanted to take time to go on retreats and study but felt he would be abandoning his earthly responsibilities. Ram Dass listened intently, nodding, and smiling gently.

In the audience, still in my judgment and sense of superiority about how much devotion I was choosing, I expected some criticism or reproach from Ram Dass. Instead, Ram Dass beamed his most tender smile as he gently told the man, "Don't worry, we'll wait." Tears flowed from the questioner and from many of us. Then Ram Dass looked out to the expectant eager faces that hungered for acknowledgment and reminded us, "None of us go Home until we all go Home."

Chastened and embarrassed at my judgment, over the next year I listed the characteristics that showed limitation and victim thinking and the ones which represented wholeness and wholeheartedness. Determined to discover what still held me back and what would demonstrate sovereignty, I saw these qualities not as either/or but as heading in a more holistic direction. I wanted to feel sovereign, lit from within, not at the mercy of reaction to outside circumstances or people. Each time I honestly evaluated my reactions and responses, I increased my capacity to be a witness, take a breath if necessary, and choose the path of greatest light.

I asked myself the question: what qualities would we need to choose and embody to create a world of peace, harmony, and abundance for all? These are the qualities I believe would change our world from one of power over to a world of empowered love.

As the Dalai Lama has reminded us, "It is very difficult to change the world one person at a time, but it is the only way." Another spiritual teacher, Owen Waters, suggests, "Your greatest service to humanity is, paradoxically, to focus on your own spiritual growth."

Then there is Mother Teresa who reminded us, "Prayer without action is no prayer at all."

What is a soul on the journey to do? I look at it as not an either/or equation; more like a teeter-totter where the balance lies in taking care of ourselves, then offering the best of our love into the world. The still point or balance requires constant correction. Think of a pilot doing their best to stay on the course. Statistics suggest about 10% of the time they are exactly on course, and the other 90% they are correcting the course! I remind myself of that whenever I realize I have become judgmental or apathetic.

Discernment is important and so is openness. I seldom question Mother Mary any longer.

Still, sometimes her suggestions are completely illogical. In San Francisco for a Wisdom University conference, I was staying at a modest hotel. As I came downstairs, to enjoy the included breakfast, Mother Mary insisted I walk down the street to the Hyatt hotel. I hesitated. Why should I spend $25 for a breakfast I would not be able to finish? Still after a moment's hesitation, I made my way to the Hyatt.

The Hostess escorted me all the way around the huge dining room to the back corner. As I sat down, I noticed two women from Australia I had met the day before sitting at an adjacent table. They nodded and invited me to join them. We chatted about the conference and what had led us to Wisdom University. Then I felt Mother Mary. Uncertain, I felt a bit embarrassed because I did not know these women nor how they might react. Nonetheless, I took a breath and told them I had a message from Mother Mary if they wanted to hear it. A little startled, they nodded their assent. To the first woman Mother Mary said you have a future working with labyrinths. To the other Mary said your future includes financial wellbeing and opportunities to connect with many people all over the world.

Finished with breakfast, we headed over to the conference. I was proud of myself for not being afraid, and yet I had no idea what the far-reaching import of these messages would be. In the months to come I would learn that the woman invited to learn about labyrinths became incredibly involved in the Labyrinth Society. Not only that, she was also guided to create a public labyrinth in Sydney, Australia. The land was donated. The landscape architect donated his time. The city encouraged the project. Now Centennial Park Labyrinth is a place of peace and refuge for all to enjoy. The second woman went on to be an executive in a multinational financial company dedicated to environmental projects and solutions around the world. It might have happened anyway. I do believe that Mary's encouragement held a light up for each of them.

Humbled, I offered a prayer of thanks to have been part of delivering a message that had such profound repercussion. It is these moments that give me courage and make me smile to know that when we speak up as we are guided, miracles often unfold.

My friend from Australia, offers this perspective on The Centennial website: "The labyrinth is a form of maze therapy offering us the opportunity to experience ourselves as vessels through which power flows, rather than seeing power as something external to self. It is a paradigm within which we can access real power. The power of our essential nature. Not power over, which is the obsession of the maze, but power with. A mutually expansive sharing of the destiny of our world.

So how do we know if we are living in a labyrinth or a maze? It is all a matter of perspective. When we feel lost and confused, we have turned our path into a maze. The signs are anxiety, comparison, and a need to control things. The myth of the maze is that it is real, that there is no alternative. When we surrender to fear, we build walls and create dead ends. We can only be free when we accept our experience and see how it might be transformed into something useful; when we realized that what is in the way, is the way. We are the alchemists of our own lives and the lead with which that alchemist is working and we are the gold it becomes."

So how do we go from guarded to guided? Practice, practice, practice.! It is not always unicorns, rainbows, and roses. Popular books suggest the secret to manifesting the car, house, job, lover of your dreams is to simply focus on what you want and write it down and repeat often. If that worked we would have lots of happily married millionaires. As a long-time spiritual coach and guide, the first thing I tell my clients is that I am not a fan of what I have dubbed "Santa Claus spirituality."

The real measure of our life and our work here as a soul is to dismantle the programming that robs us of our innocence and our intuition. When we have enough clarity and confidence to connect with our golden stream of light from the Creator/Source, there is an igniting of our purpose, passion, and possibilities. The seven gateways is one map of our body/mind/emotions that we can use to facilitate this process. Each chakra stores old ideas, hurt, and traumas until we face, embrace, and heal old wounds. I would love to say this clearing is completed and from then on we are "done." Au contraire: it is not so. New challenges come, new discoveries are offered and always, more surrender is required. Let me share one more personal experience that required me to let go of being guarded and just be guided.

In a small, lovely church on Maui where I had stopped in to say a prayer, I was given the next assignment that would challenge me to more discovery, and surrender. On that quiet afternoon, as I bowed my head in the sweet peace of the sanctuary, Mary came through clearly and said it was time to bring forth a new form of Reiki. It would be called Manna Reiki. Manna was the bread that God had provided on a daily basis to the Israelites on their long journey through the desert.

Surprised at this request, since I had been trained in such a traditional manner, I was conflicted. Why would we need another form of Reiki? Mary said that as our bodies had changed and our responsibilities increased to become sovereign, the old form of Reiki no longer offered all of the light needed. This would be an inner alignment Reiki so that each practitioner would be able to hold and carry a pristine, congruent energy field. Precious, pristine, present, they would be open to the breath of Spirit filling them each day.

Back in my hotel room, I closed my eyes and meditated, asking to connect with the spirit of Dr. Usui (the founder of traditional Usui Reiki) to confirm that this next step had his blessing. The room filled with his strength and humor, and I wrote down what he said. "Dearest Emissary of Light, it is time to marry the energy of light with the energy of love. In my time there was so much darkness and doubt that light was needed to dispel. Love in the way you have found with Mary was not possible in bodies that still held so much denial. The radiance of Reiki, along with so many energy modalities have illuminated many. Now in the space that still divides the world from sovereignty you and others can help to bring about the long-awaited union of feminine and masculine."

Subdued, excited, and curious, I wondered just what this would mean. It would be two years of silence before the next step appeared.

My monthly radio show on Blog Talk radio regaled listeners with Mary's wisdom and humor. Callers could ask her questions and she would direct them to see obstacles morph into new possibilities. As our time wound to an end, to my immense surprise, Mary dramatically announced, "Now Samarah will bring forth a new form of Reiki. If you feel called, write to her and she will come."

My mouth dropped open. What? I had not received any further information after the initial download in Maui. It had been two years. What had just happened?

Sure enough, the next day I had an email from a woman in California who said she wanted to take this new Reiki and had three other interested friends; so, when could I come? Feeling the call and sticking to my statement that I would go where I was invited, we arranged a time later that month. When she asked me how much the class would be, I took a breath and out of my mouth came $333 for the weekend. The numbers would reflect the union of head, heart, and hands, the inner trinity.

Certain that I would be told just what to include, I meditated each day as the time drew near for my departure. Nothing, Zero. Zilch. Talk about surrender and trust. As a former teacher I wanted my lesson plan, my curriculum, my materials to be prepared. Nothing. As I packed to leave I gathered my traditional materials to bring and stuffed them into my carryon so I could make notes on the plane.

Once in the air, I opened my carryon to review the Usui curriculum I had taught dozens of times. It was only then that I heard, "You will not need any of these." This would be the next test of my willingness to show up, be present, and trust that what needed to come through would come through!

After a restless night, I met my eager participants the next day. I had asked each of them to bring a picture of someone that was important to them, along with any crystals or objects they would like to have as part of our altar. I brought a pareo from Hawaii for the alter cloth, depicting whales and dolphins, ocean and hibiscus flowers, my idea of heaven on earth. We began by standing in a circle and calling in all of the Reiki family, as well as our own angels and guides.

Taking a breath and letting go of the previous fully prepared teaching model, I began by telling them I truly had no idea what would happen next as this was the first class in a whole new kind of Reiki. To my great relief, they were all excited rather than disappointed!

Glancing at the altar, I was guided to ask them to introduce themselves by sharing whose picture they had brought with them and why. This gave us a common ground of understanding each other and who they honored and loved. Thankfully, Mother Mary had guided me as she now came through to share more about what this Reiki was and how it could help them align whatever had been disparate, wounded, separate.

My beloved Emissaries of Light, thank you for your courage in coming to this next initiation of your light. There will be three attunements. The first I will offer to heal your hearts of betrayal and judgment. With your purity restored, you can now offer and receive the breadth and depth of love that is here for you.

Archangel Metatron will offer the next initiation. He will work to clear your human mind and connect fully with your divine mind. No longer wracked by doubt and self-criticism, or held captive by the world's constraints, you will see the path of light that is yours and embrace it.

The third initiation will be with Archangel Michael. Here you will be given the sword of truth to cut past all illusion, and the shield of light so that you may go wherever you are guided in safety.

As Mary finished speaking, I opened my eyes and looked around the room. There was a hushed expectancy on the face of each of the women. How could I go on when I had never channeled Metatron or Michael? I could just give them back their money and head home. What was I doing? I felt Mother Mary's reassurance. **"Breathe, daughter breathe, we would not have brought you here only to abandon you.** Then, each woman stood, and Mary touched their hearts and transmitted a healing blast of unconditional love.

Taking another deep breath, and standing to feel more in control, I asked Metatron to come through for the highest good of all. I felt him join first with my energy and then take over. He began to pace around the room, bent over as if he were carrying too heavy a load.

Buts, you carry all your buts like hats one on top of

the other until you cannot stand up!

You say I would do that, But. I could try that But, every time you get a great idea or a promising opportunity, before you move one step, the hats begin to pile up and soon you sit back down, weary, overcome and now too burdened to continue. Are you ready to let them go and be free?

The group was nodding and laughing at Metatron's antics. One by one he had them sit and agree to be free and then with a swoop he had them cast aside any hats they still wore and stand free and ready to go wherever their souls guided them.

The final attunement with Archangel Michael took us back to a long-ago time when we each had pledged our willingness to come at this critical juncture when as Mary had told us there was the most to gain and the most to lose. We stood in a circle and promised to have courage and to walk wherever we were guided.

The day was drawing to a close and I suggested we each go home and journal about the day and be ready for the next when we would share how we wanted to walk in the world from now on. It had been a day full of joy and deep gratitude that I had trusted and surrendered.

The next day was full of sharing, much laughter a bit of fun, and even some dancing. I was gratified that all of the women said they had gained more clarity and wanted to know when I might offer the next level. Word spread of this triple Reiki alignment, and I was invited to share it with dozens of willing folks over the next three years. I developed Manna 2 and Manna 3 and then came White Star Reiki with a link to our galactic nature.

Discovery is not one gateway. As we keep moving on our path of light, doors keep opening. One afternoon as I was meditating about the White Star and its meaning, I was shown it was Venus, the planet of love. Smiling at this idea, Mother Mary offered the next challenge.

Daughter of light, we would like you to train 22 White Star Reiki Master teachers just as Mrs. Takata trained her twenty-two. From there, over time, there can be many thousands.

Amused at this potential assignment, I conveyed my message back to Mary. "You know I live in Cornville, right?" My tiny town has less than five thousand people and up until that point, I had trained everyone in person. Still, I said yes and put out the call. It is now 2021 and I have trained 17 White Star Reiki Masters! I developed a yearlong program they could complete online with the final attunements in person at a glorious Sedona retreat or a special spot they chose

In 2022 I will be co-teaching with my first White Star Master who just completed Reiki 3 with her students, five of whom want to become Masters. All of this from my Cornville home where I said yes and did not say "But!"

The rewards I have received from my commitment to be an Emissary of Light are profound and numerous. I author this book knowing there are more of us. Whether your path is with Mother Mary or any face of love, whether you are a

Reiki fan or find joy in something else, my prayer is that you choose the path of love that brings you deep peace and lasting joy. My prayer is that you give and receive the blessings of this life. I will end with a poem I wrote that is a call to Common Ground.

May you walk in beauty, bounty, blessings, and aloha.

Samarah Grace

A Call to Common Ground

This is a time of chaos.
This is a time for
healing. This is a time
of choice.
This is a time to care.
This is a time to stand and say
"Yes!" This is a time to stand and
say "No!"
This is a time of
challenge.
This is a time for peace.
We join together, old and young, frail and strong, hearts and
hands To heal the wounds, we have wrought for centuries.
There is blood in our waters, acid in our lands, death in our skies.
We join together to take up the sword of truth and the shield of
light.
To dissolve all boundaries, deceit, and judgment,
To stand united once again, I and thou, in the garden
of Brotherhood.
The human heart is Common Ground.

About Samarah Grace

 A world-renowned conscious channel, Samarah Grace is a skilled Reiki Master Teacher, and gifted spiritual guide. Clairaudient since childhood, a visitation from Mother Mary catapulted Samarah into an extraordinary global journey, sharing Mary's wisdom and healing presence. Samarah holds a Doctor of Ministry degree in Wisdom Spirituality and draws from diverse traditions to assist people in hearing and trusting their own soul guidance, to create lives of passion, purpose, and radiant wellbeing. www.samarahgrace.com

Made in the USA
Las Vegas, NV
02 December 2021

35877889R00105